Lost History

Vancouver Street Art in 1985

by Ron Kearse

Second Edition – September 2015

ISBN 978-1-927848-19-7 (Soft Cover)

Published by

Filidh Publishing

Victoria, British Columbia

Lost History

Vancouver Street Art in the 1980's

Street art, look at it closely. Far from being an eyesore it is a moment in time, a reflection, a snapshot, a hammer. Some of it is political, some angry, some observational and some just downright artistic expression. It is social statement and history. Who are these guerilla artists, these midnight Rembrandts, these magicians?

In the mid-1980's, my Yashica 35 mm camera became my trusty sidekick. Armed with several rolls of black and white film we traveled around Vancouver capturing the street art at that time. This is the Vancouver that is on the verge of great change. All of this leading up to the year 1986 when the world's fair, Expo 86 arrived in our city… and Vancouver would never be the same again. Here is some of what my camera and I captured.

Ron Kearse

September 2013

The Orillia Block

795 Seymour St

On the corner of Robson and Seymour Streets where, what is now a glass office tower stands, there was a unique looking building called the Orillia Block. It housed a small deli, a coffee shop and was home to one of Vancouver's first gay-owned and operated bars, Twiggy's. It was opened as a private gay club in 1967 and in the 1970s; the name was changed to Faces.

In those days, liquor licenses were hard to come by for all pubs, so Faces operated as a bottle club, where patrons brought their own booze and checked it at the bar. The bartender would tag people's liquor and serve it back to them on request. Faces eventually got a special liquor license in the mid-1970s. This probably explains why the Y in the word History in the photo is in the shape of a martini glass. The club remained popular with gays and lesbians until the building was closed for demolition in 1985. The photo to the right shows what was the entrance of Faces.

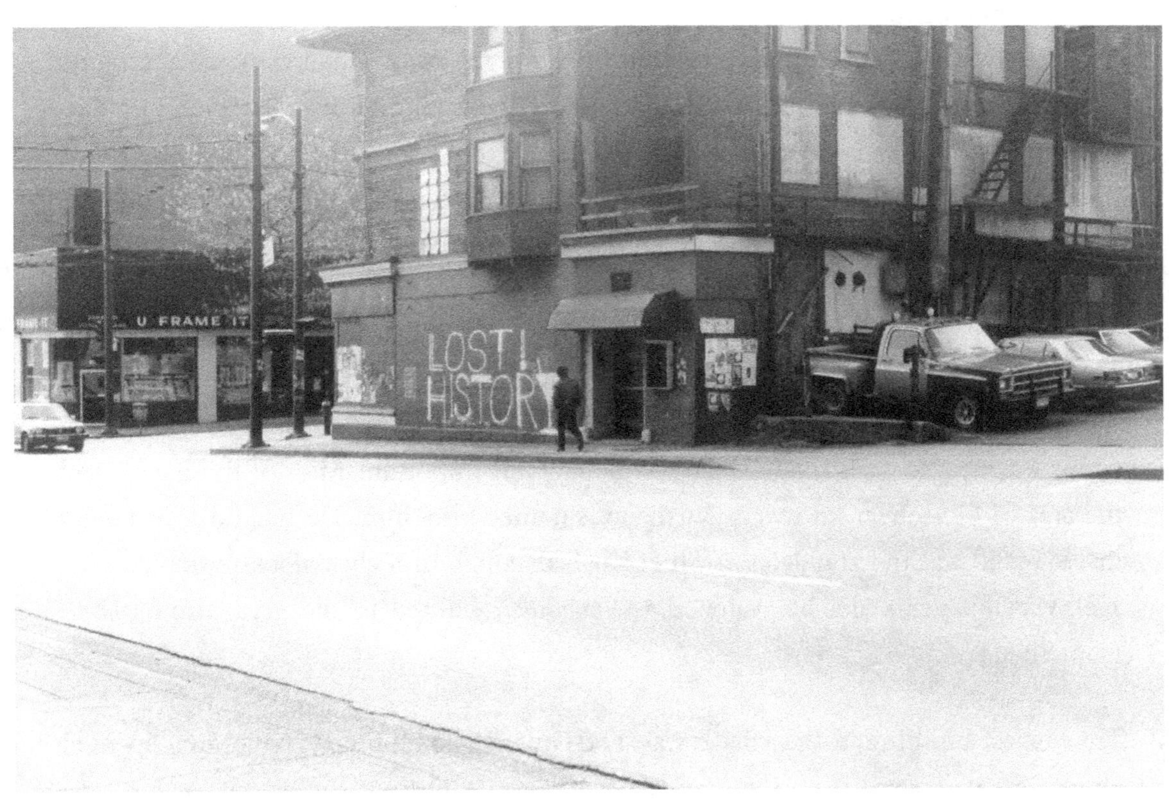
U FRAME IT
LOST!
HISTORY

Snauq

Or: Sun'ahk,

This painting to the right appeared on a support under the south side of the Burrard Bridge, and it caught my eye right away. I had assumed the name Snauq, (written along the bottom of the support), was the name of the painted Raven character. But I went to the library to do some research and discovered that until the turn of the Twentieth Century it was the name of a First Nations village, which stood where the south end of the Burrard Bridge now exists.

When the British ship HMS Plumper first surveyed the English Bay area in 1859, Snauq was already well established. It became a thirty-seven acre reserve created by the colonial government of James Douglas for the Squamish First Nation. Snauq's last Chief was August Jack Khatsalahno (which means Important Man of the Lake), and the area of Vancouver known as Kitsilano is named after him. He was born in Snauq in 1876 and was the grandson of Chief Khatsalanough of S'cheethloos. When August Jack was ten years old, he watched as Vancouver burned in the great fire of 1886 from Snauq.

The biggest building in the village was The Great Potlatch house; which was located about 250 yards east from the end of what is now Chestnut Street, facing the West End. It was about 175 to 200 feet long, about 70 feet wide and was made of cedar planks. It had a peaked roof, dirt floor and around the inside perimeter was a platform about five feet wide – enough to sleep two people side by side. There was also a village graveyard located near the corner of what are now Cedar Street and First Avenue.

In 1913 the reserve land was sold to the CPR, and the village of Snauq was dismantled. The land has since been used as industrial reserve and an RCAF equipment depot in World War two.

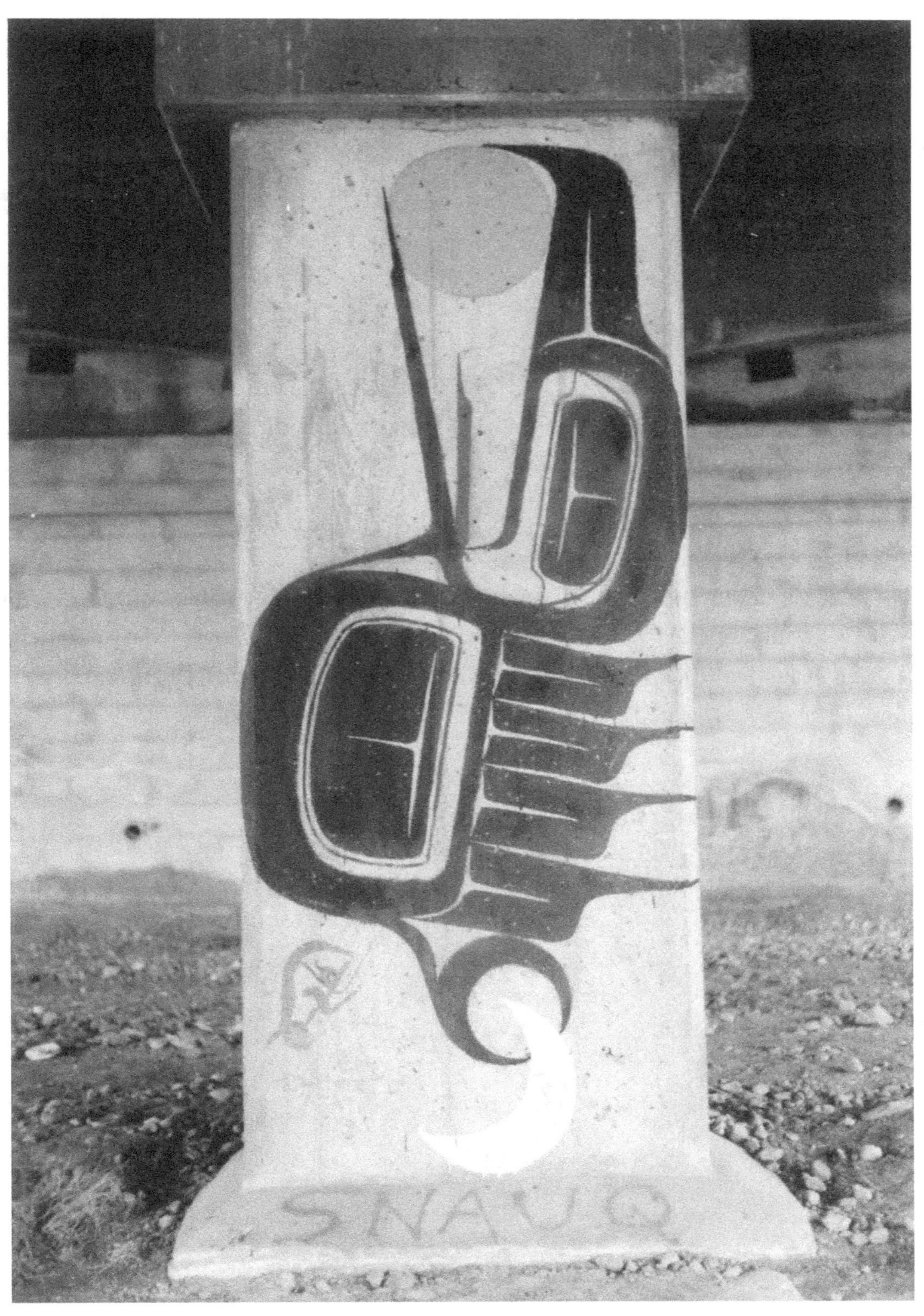
SNAUQ

This photo is of some of Snauq's inhabitants and is courtesy of the City of Vancouver Archives. From left to right: Yam-Schloot (Mary), Jericho Charlie, William Green, Peelass George (from Chilcootin), Chief Jimmy and Tow-hu-quam-kee (seated).

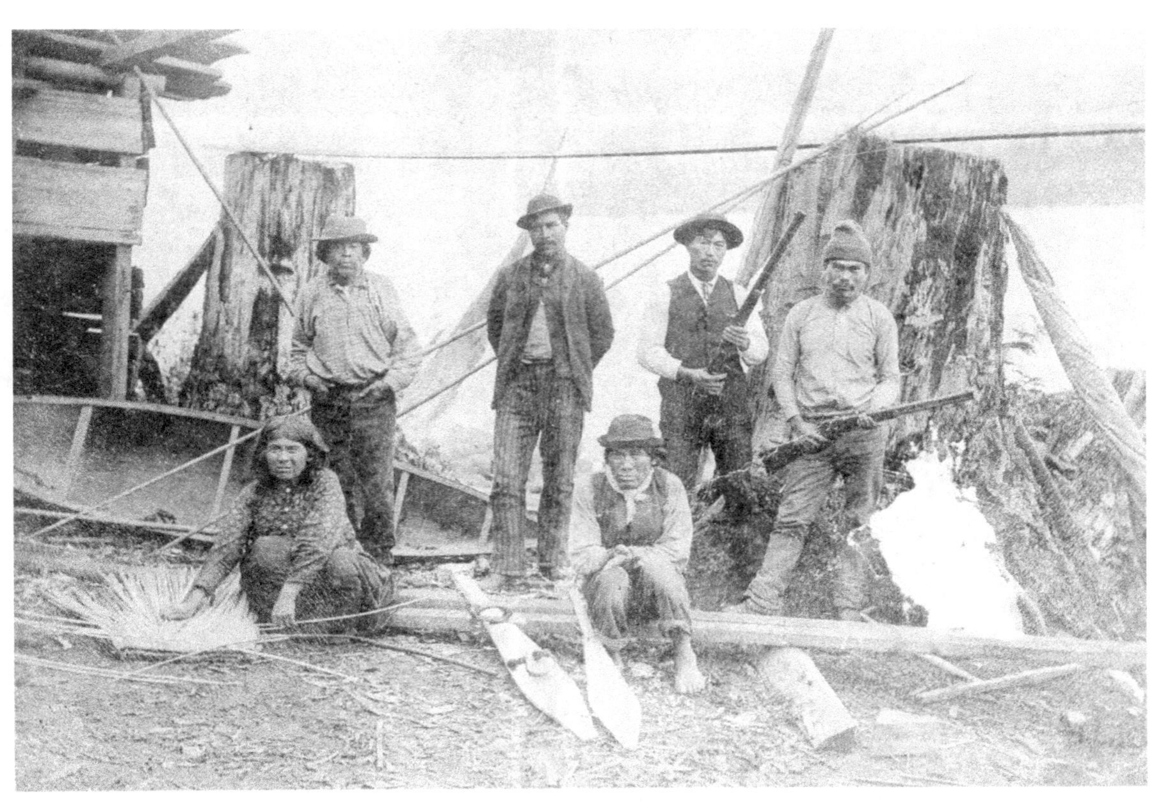

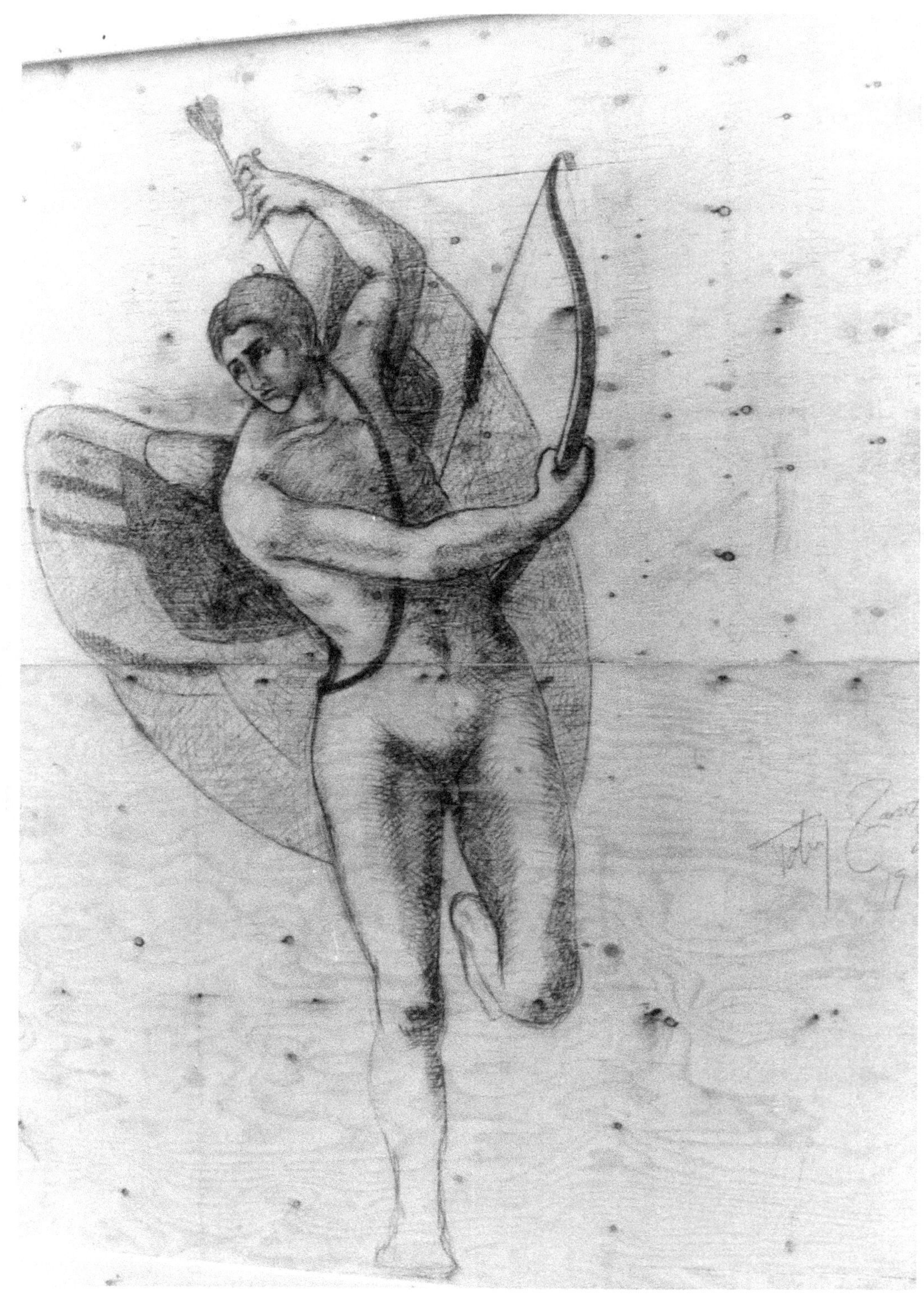

Artist Toby Jantzen

Artist: Toby Jantzen

In 1985, there was a construction site at the corner of Robson and Cardero Streets. This was to become what is now The Robson Public Market. While the construction walls were up a local artist named Toby Jantzen took it upon himself to create his own street art gallery. Mimicking the styles of: Michelangelo, Gauguin, Picasso, the Renaissance and science fiction he created his own show which was not only popular among the locals, but landed him on the front page of the Vancouver Sun, a spot on the local six o'clock TV news and a $10,000.00 grant from the Canada Council, (a tidy sum of money in those days). Jantzen eventually left Canada because the authorities were not fond of some of the chalk drawings he displayed in other public shows, and he found himself in jail a couple of time as a result. He has been living in San Francisco for many years where he makes a living as a full-time artist. Here are some of the pieces he created around that construction site all those years ago.

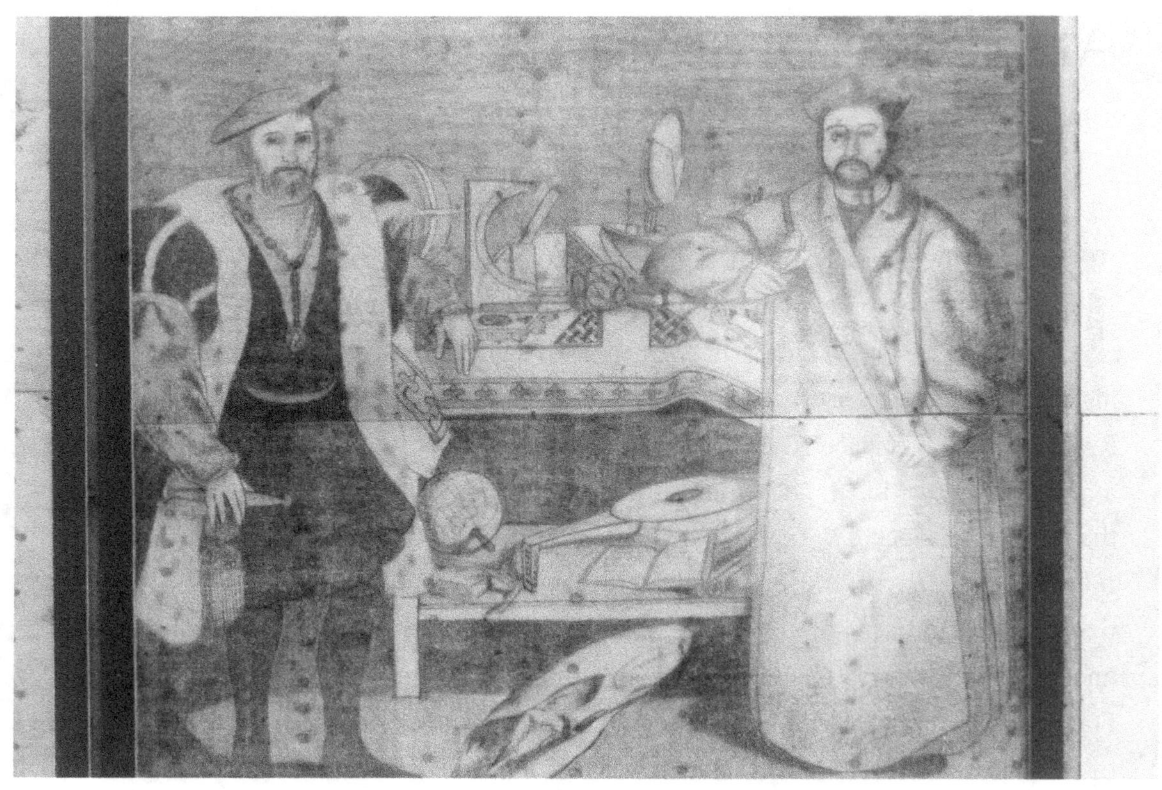

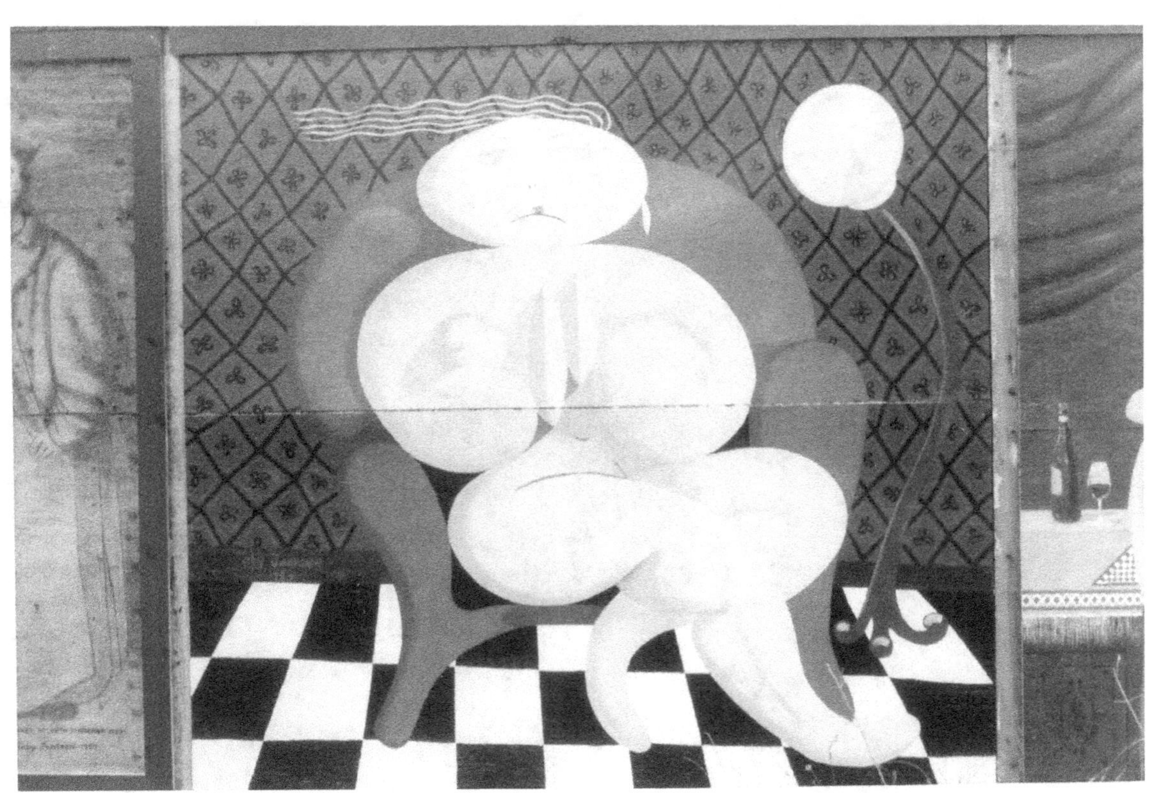

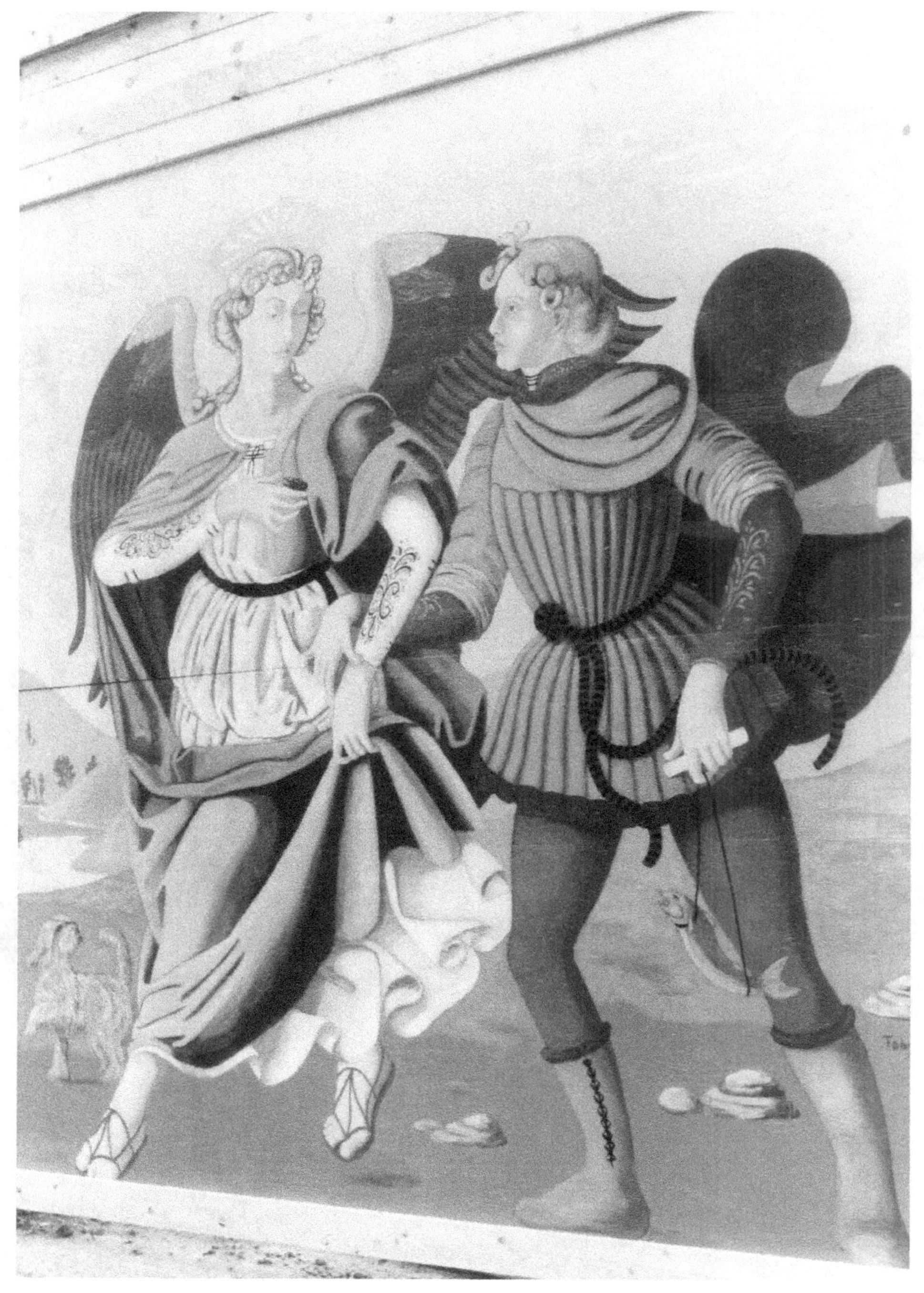

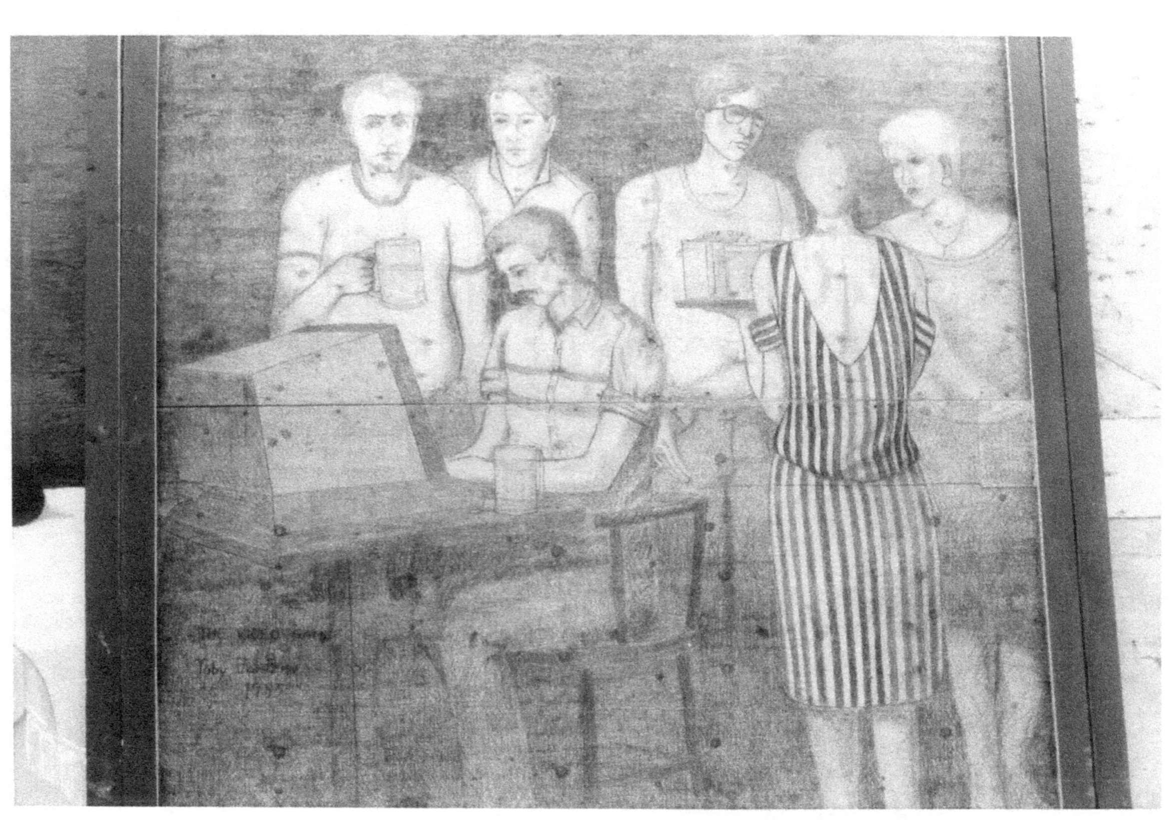

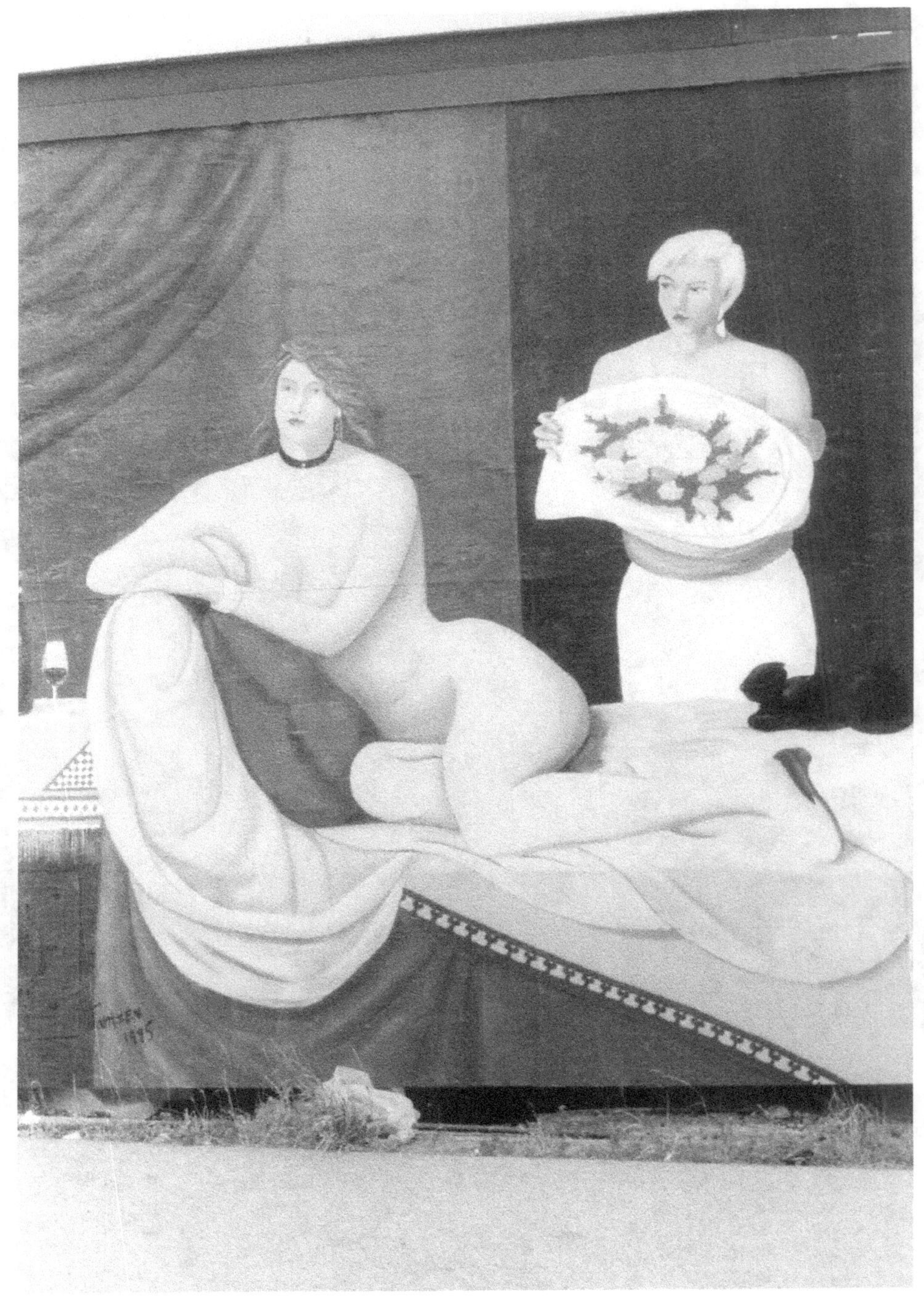

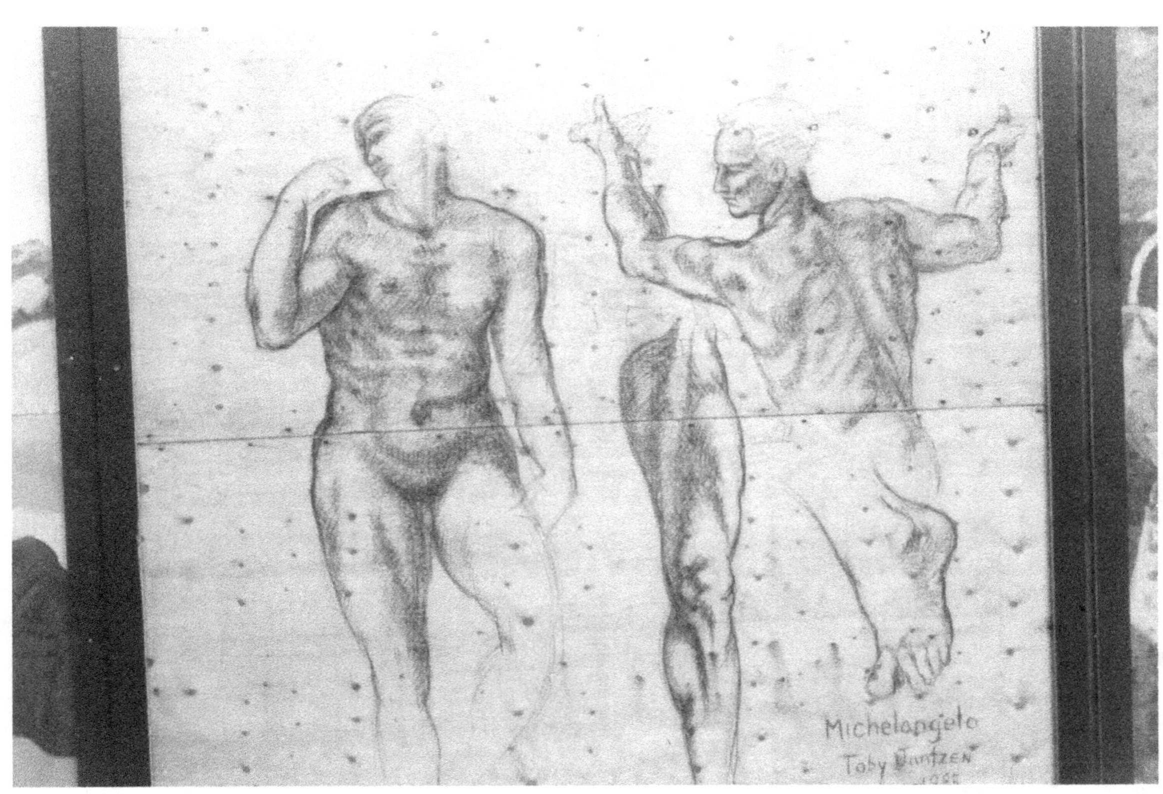
Michelangelo
Toby

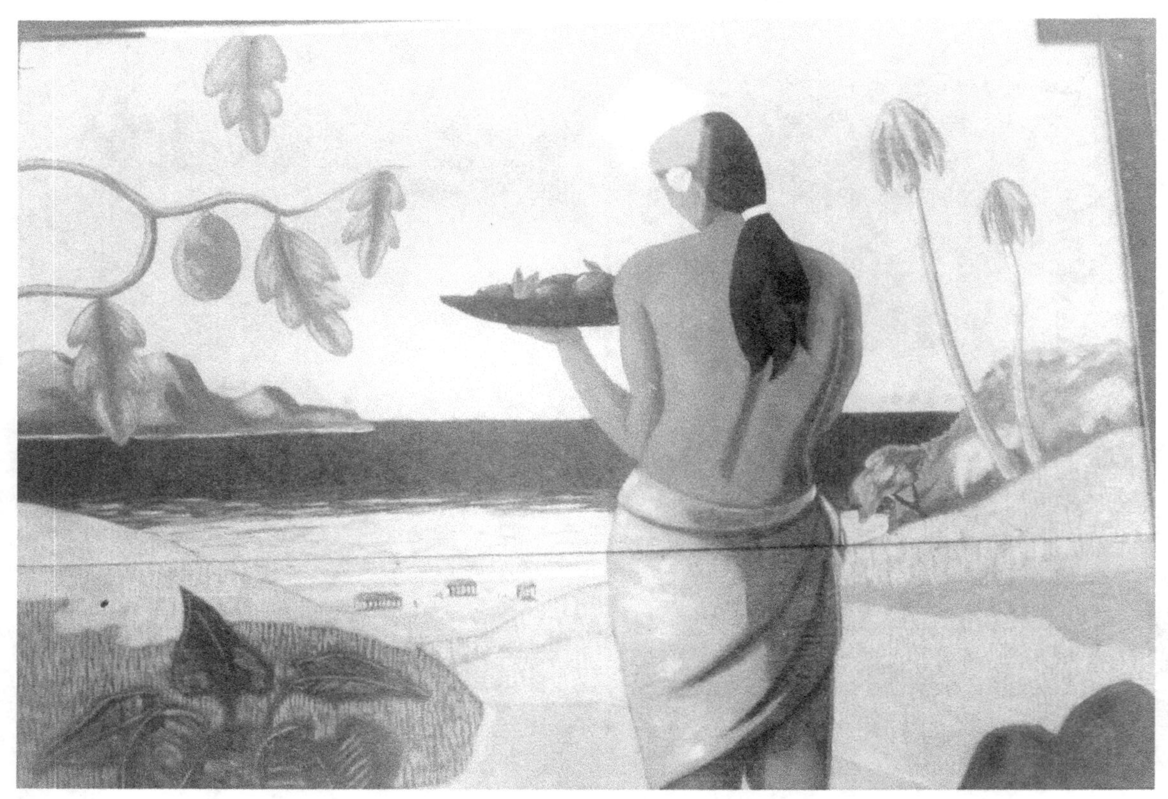

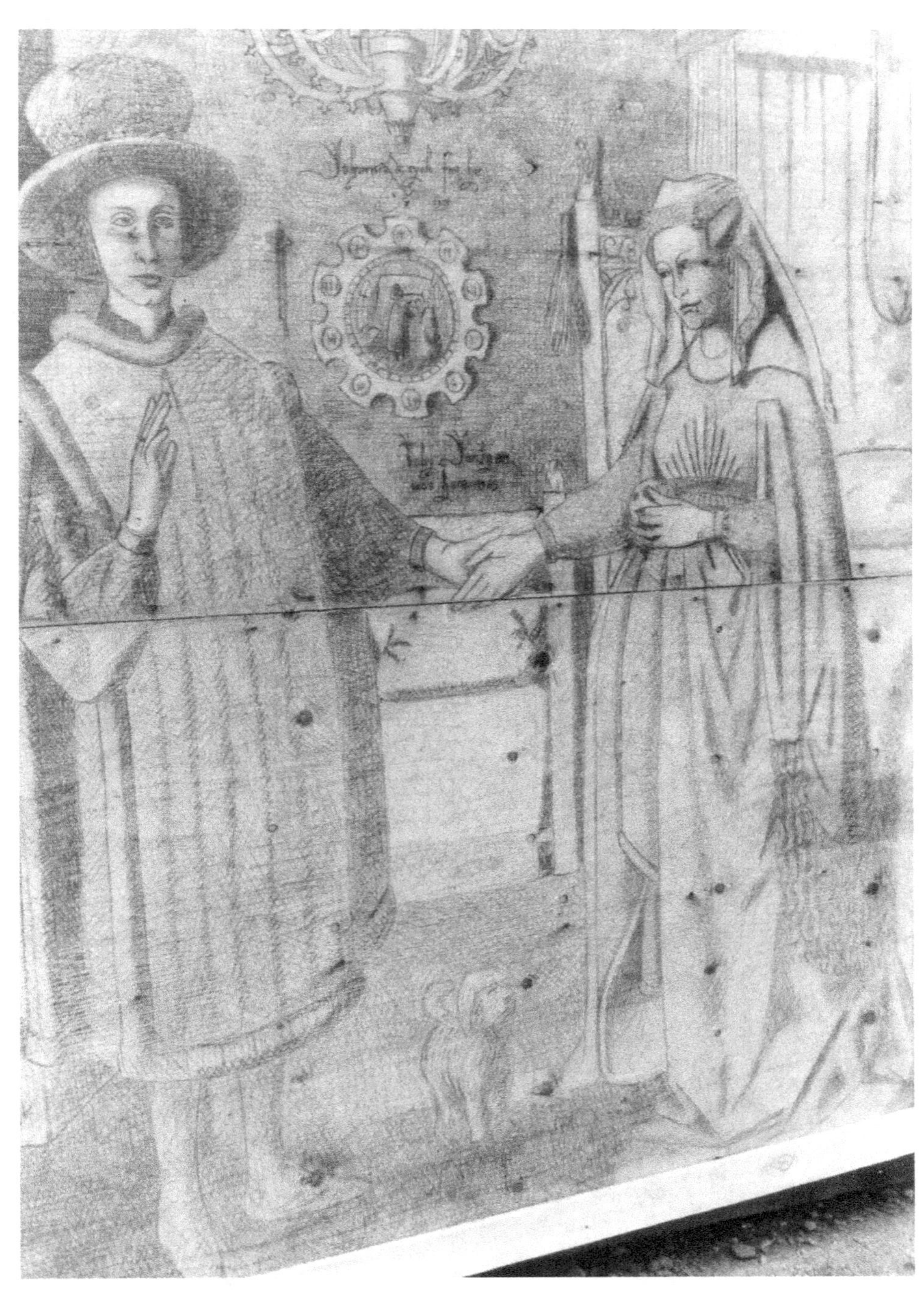

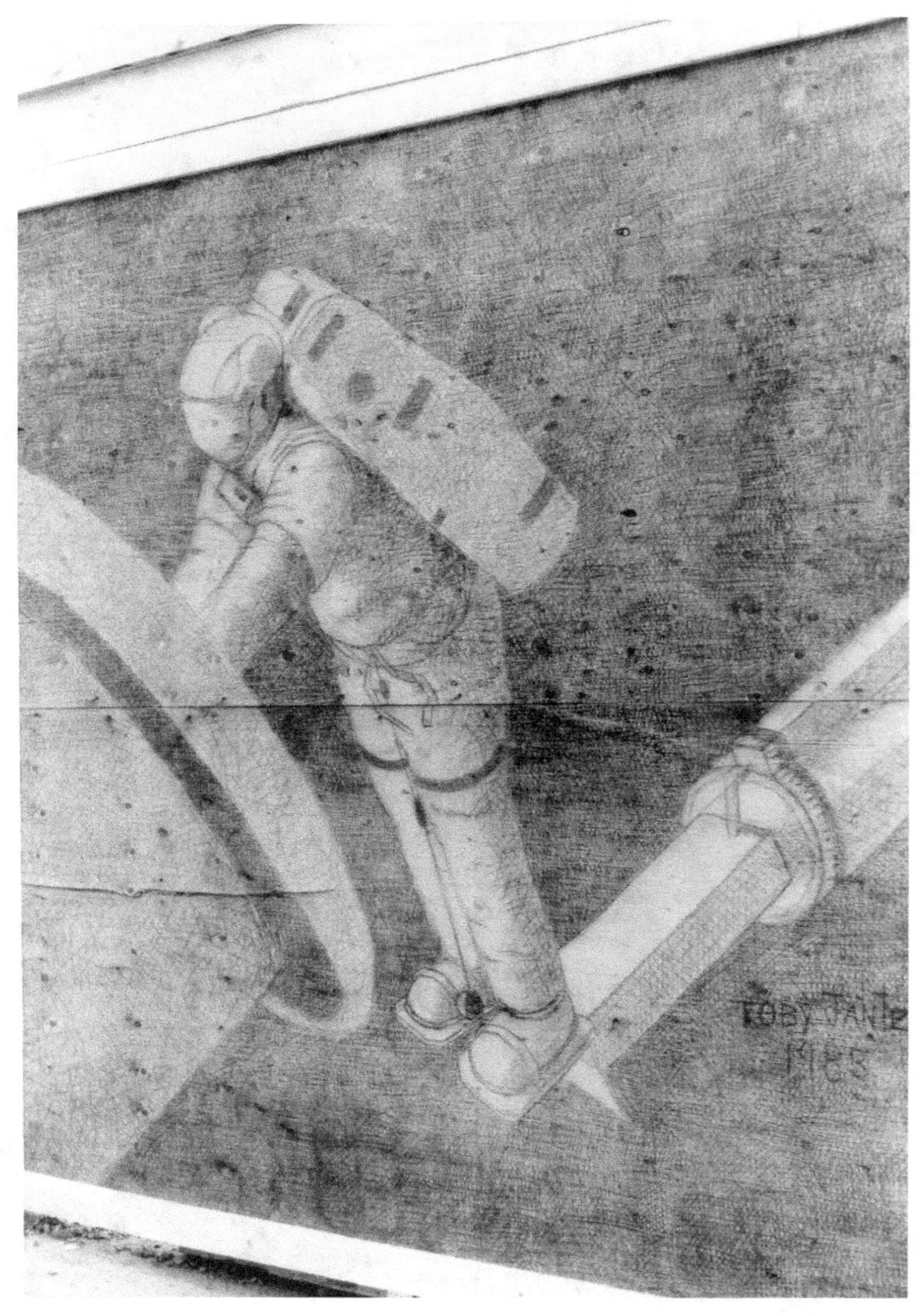

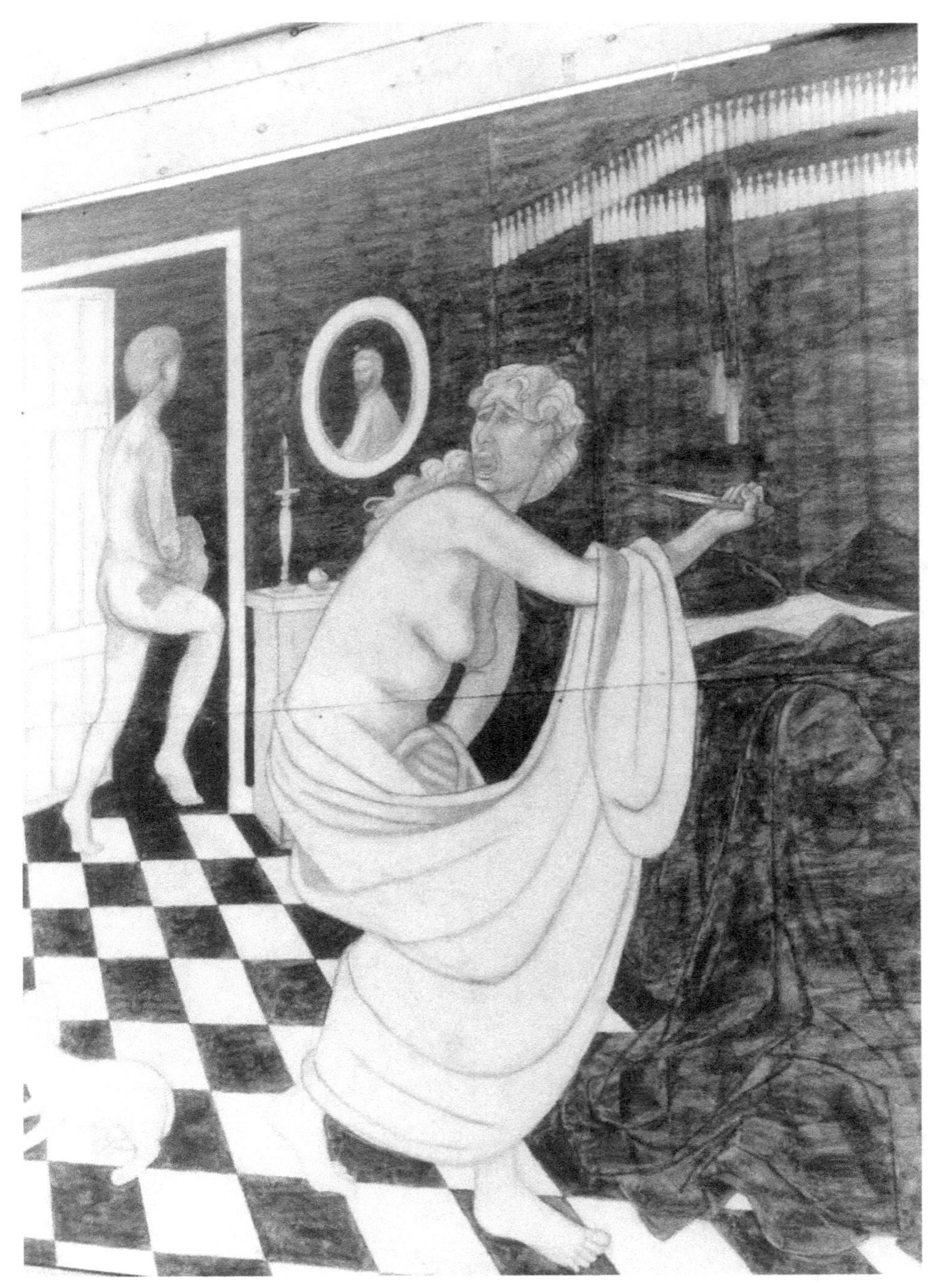

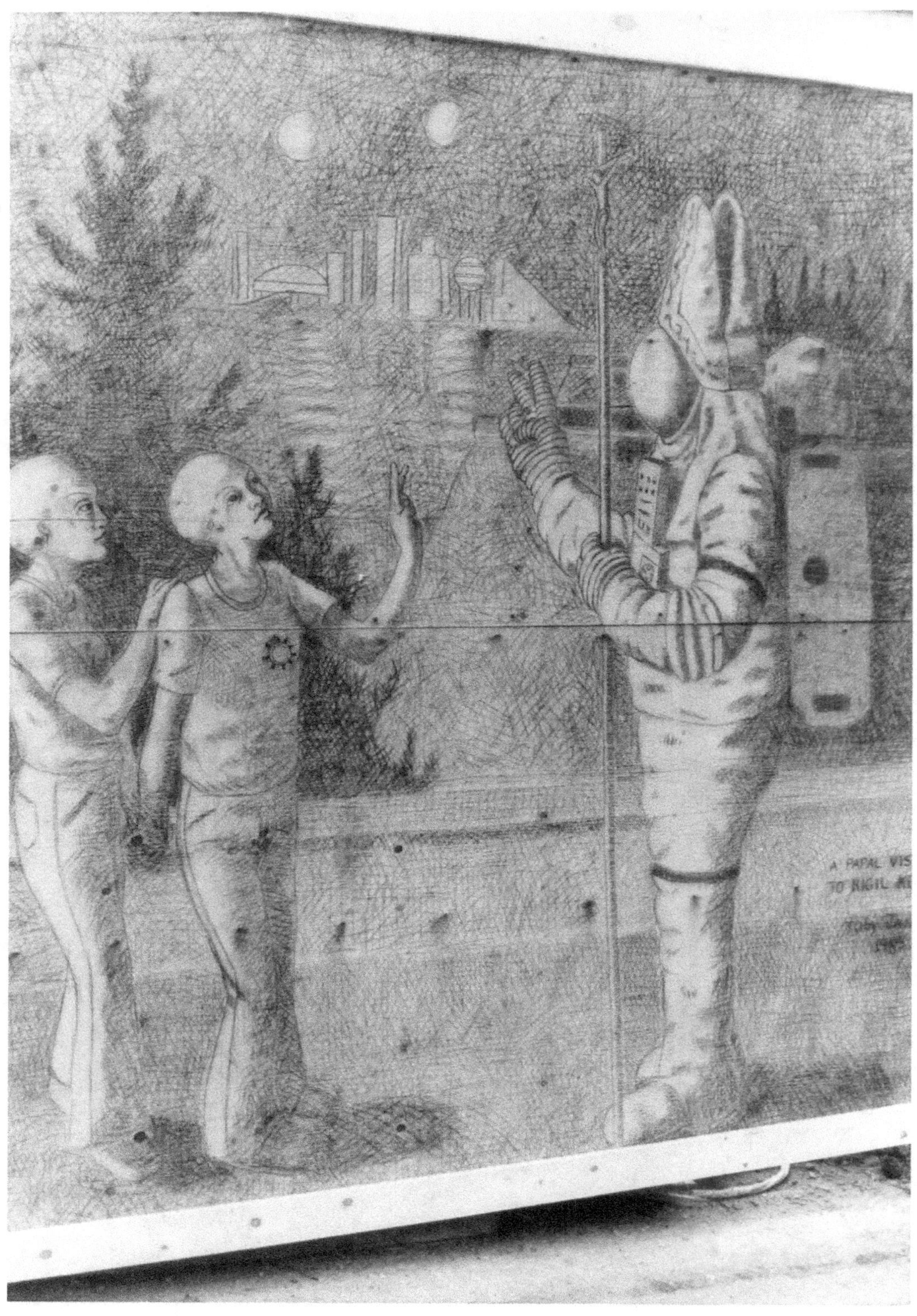
A PAPAL VIS
TO RIGIL

Artist: Pablo Fiasco

Pablo Fiasco's art was ubiquitous around Vancouver during the early eighties. He was among a handful of well-known street artists like 12 Midnite, I Blockhead and Art Wanker. You could see their works on the sides of many of the walls of the older buildings downtown. Unfortunately many of the buildings have long since disappeared, and Pablo Fiasco's art has never been seen in Vancouver again. So, what happened? Pablo was born in England and his parents immigrated to Vancouver when he was very young. He cites 12 Midnite as being the main inspiration for his art and pursued it relentlessly. Pablo Fiasco returned to England where he has made quite a name for himself and his street art around places like Brighton. He has had several shows in galleries around London and recently he has been working closely with independent musicians and slam poets.

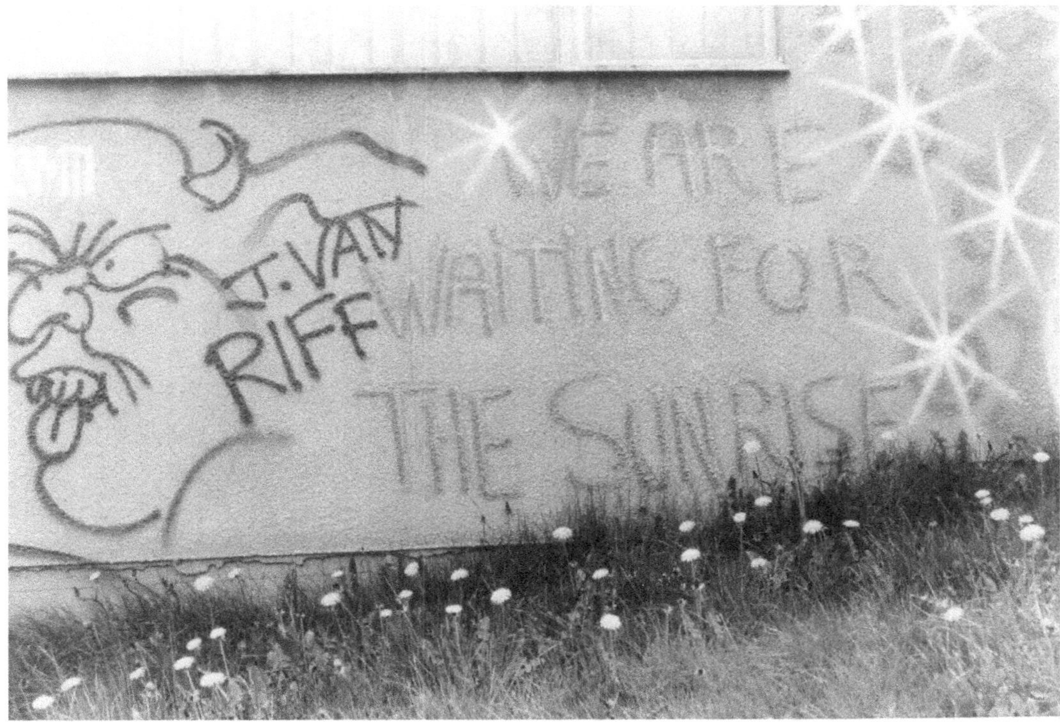

PABLO
FiASCO

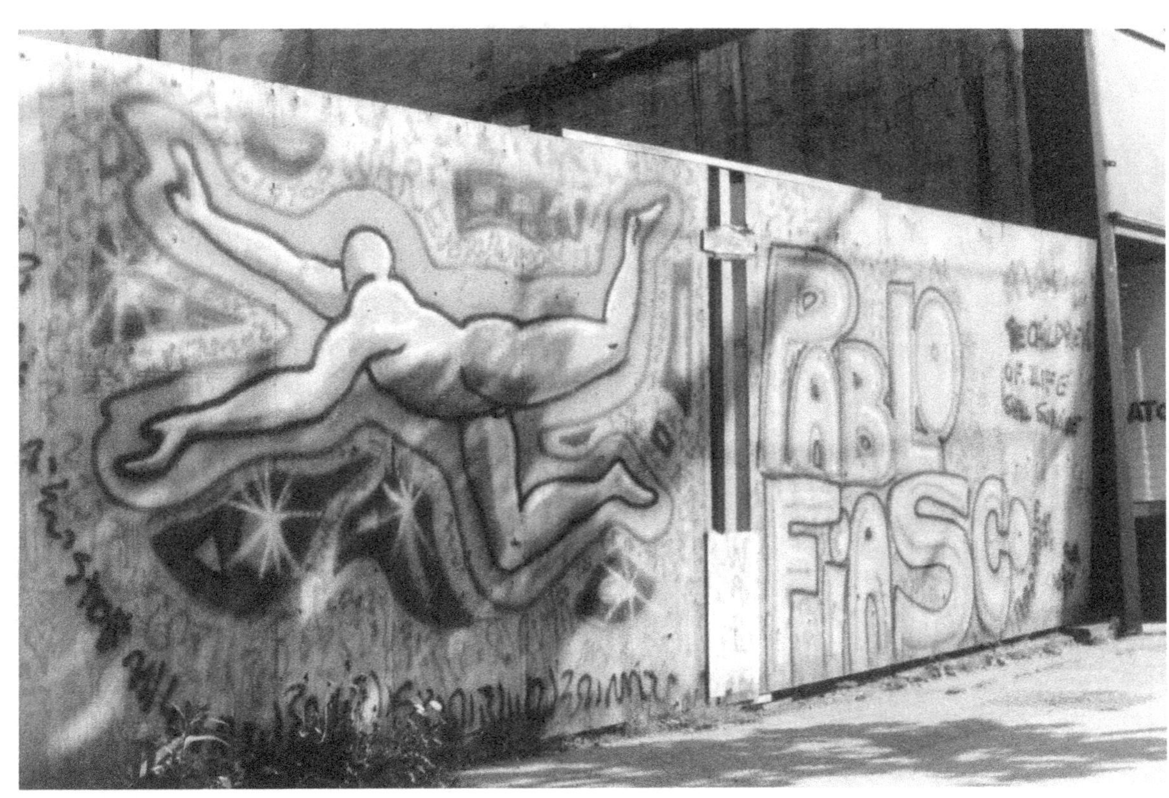
PABLO
FIASCO

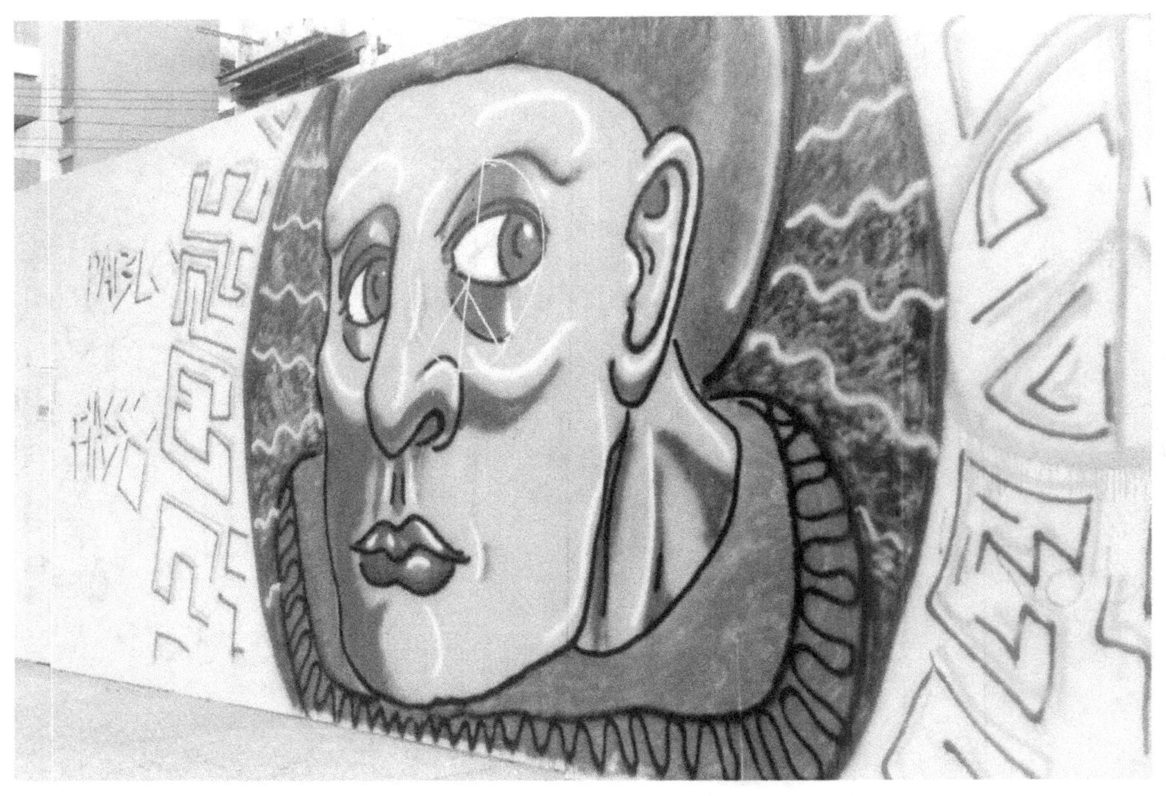

Let's not forget all of the other street artists and taggers who remain nameless, but whose creations seem to appear overnight for all of us to behold in the light of day. These pieces of commentary are too clever to be ignored. So I've included them and the locations of they were found at the time.

Homer Street between West Pender and Hastings.

Doorway on the 1200 Block Commercial Drive, (Commercial and William)

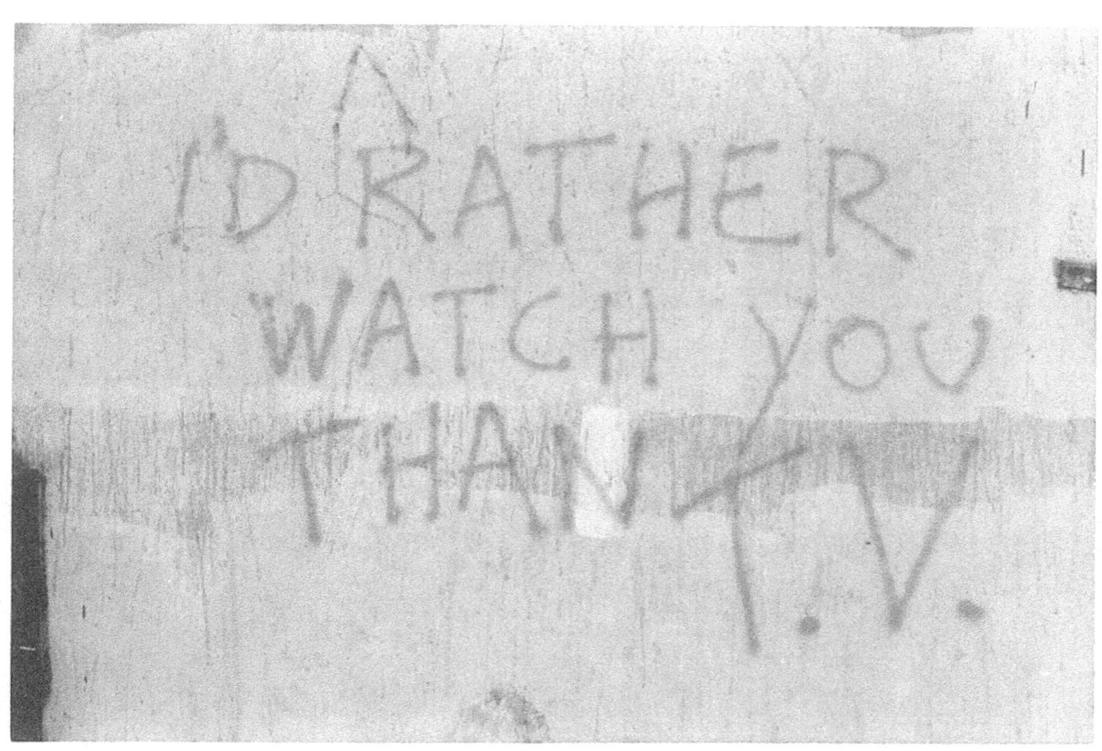

Davie Street between Hornby and Burrard.

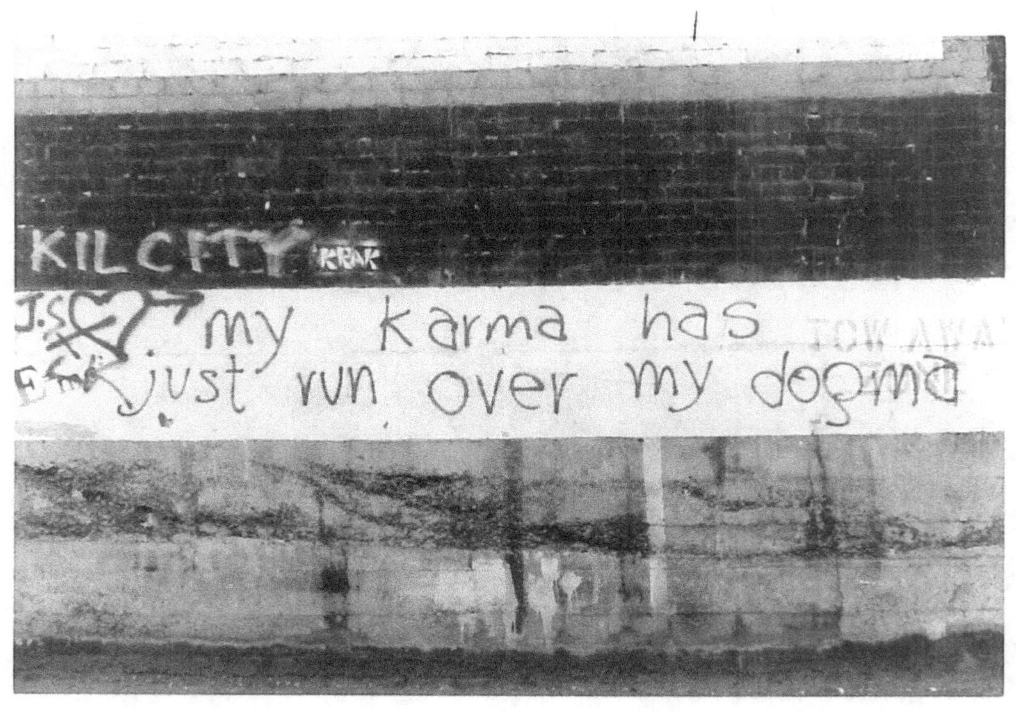

West Pender and Beatty Streets.

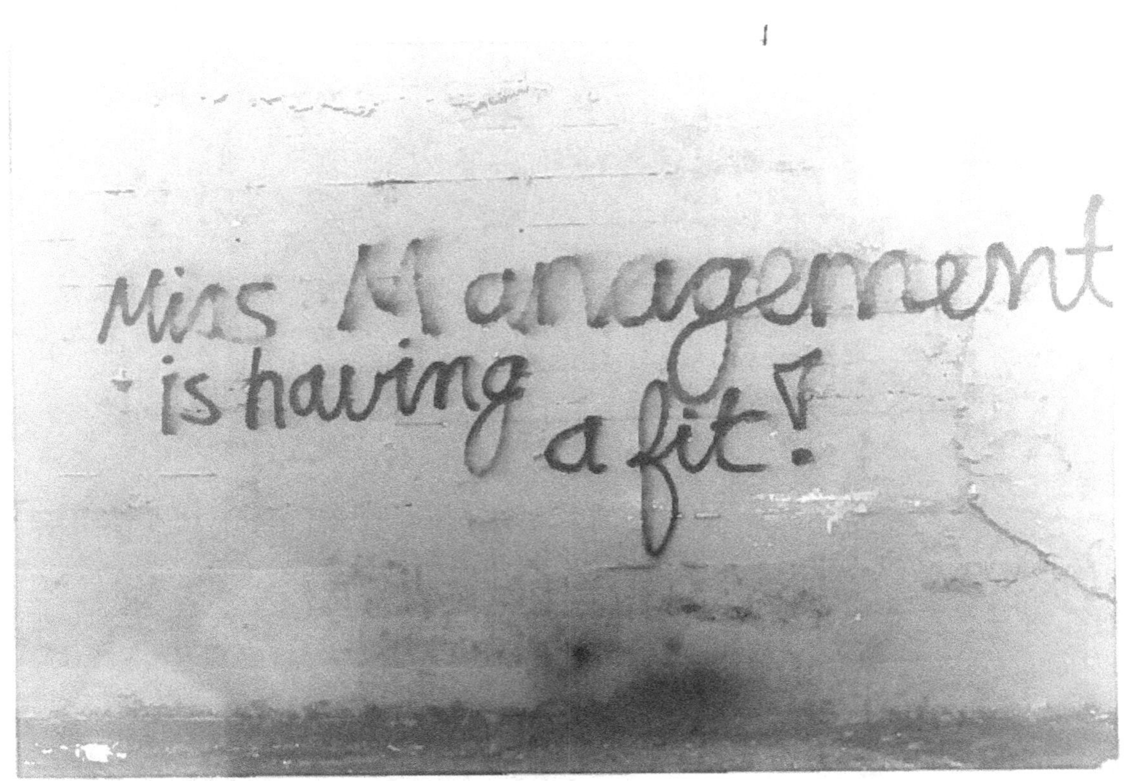

Between Dunsmuir and West Pender on Homer Street.

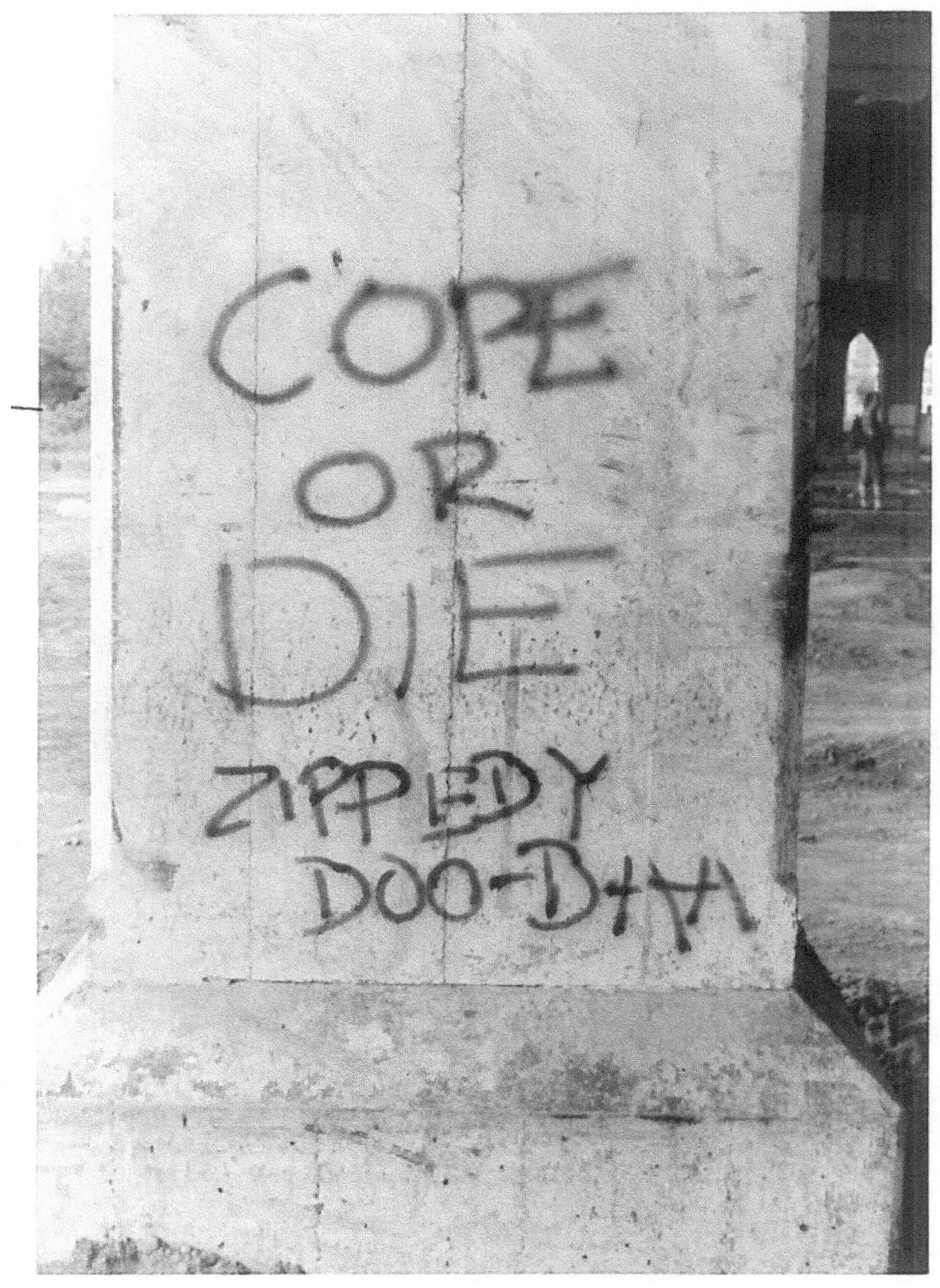

Support under the south side of the Burrard Bridge

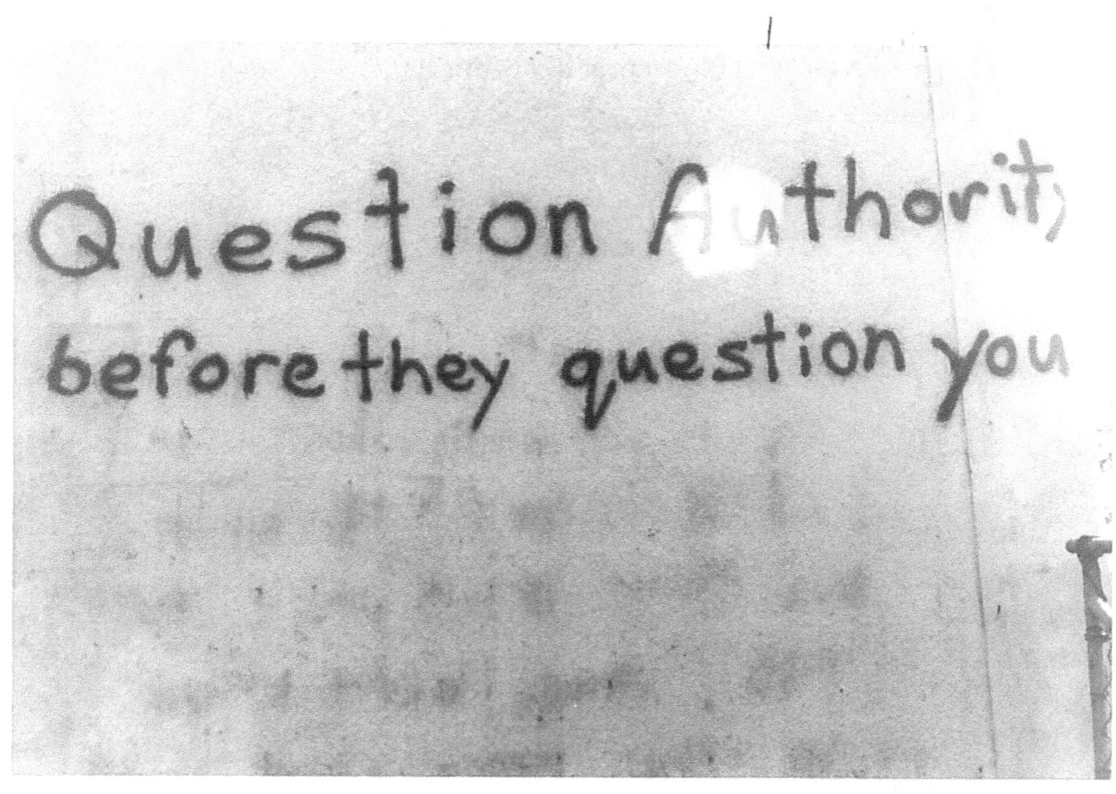

Found at 800 block Homer Street

Here are two graffiti stencils that were commonly seen in Vancouver during the early to mid-1980s: *PEACE* with broken sword, and *Spend Your Savings*. This was on West Pender near Beatty Street.

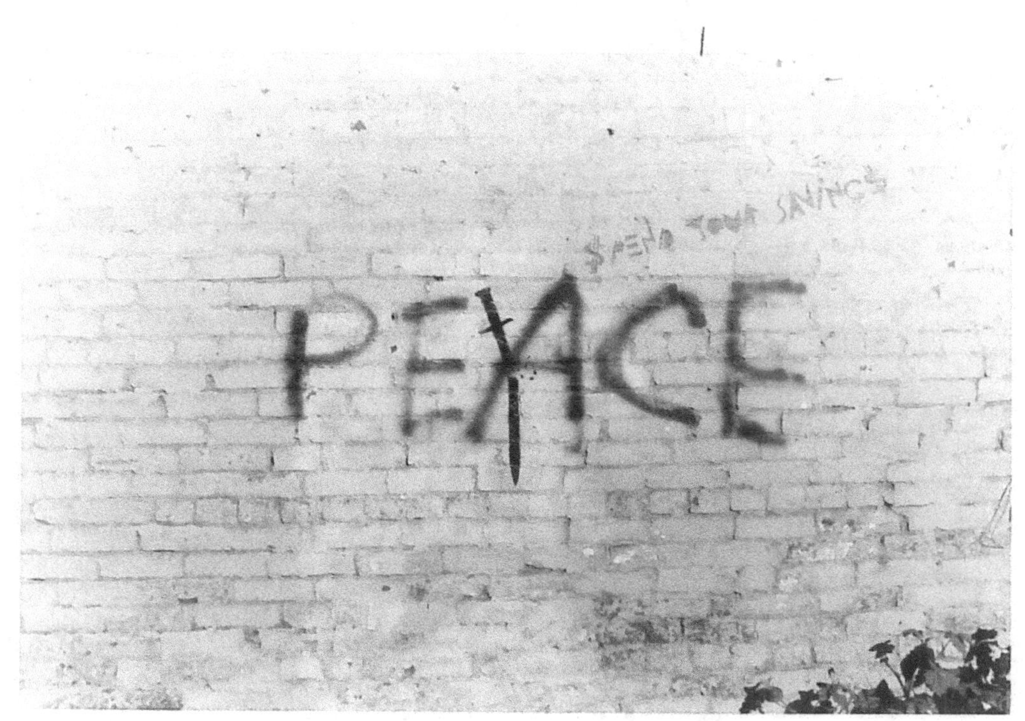

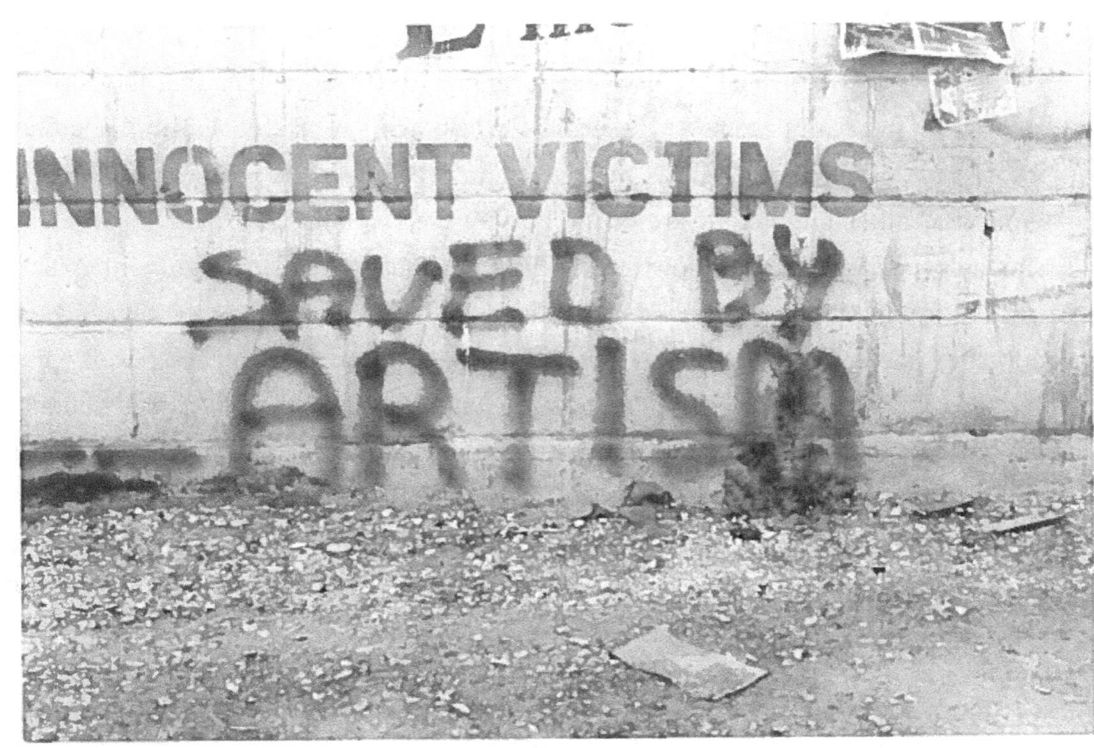

I found this in the alley between Thurlow and Burrard, Robson and Haro.

Politics

Who was Belmas? This piece of angry graffiti sprayed along the top of the wall screams at the passers-by. So here's a brief lesson in Canadian history. Juliet Belmas was part of an urban guerrilla group called Direct Action, (the other members were: Ann Hansen, Gerry Hannah, Doug Stewart and Brent Taylor). They were not motivated by ideology, but rather frustration with a lack of results from traditional methods of activism. They believed that by engaging in action, they could jolt others to act as well. So they set upon launching a series of what they called, "actions" around British Columbia and Ontario; which included vandalizing the headquarters of AMAX Mining Company and the offices of the BC Ministry of Environment. They bombed the BC Hydro Cheekye-Dunsmuir Substation on Vancouver Island causing five million dollars damage, and then they bombed Litton Industries in Toronto, (Litton was said to be responsible for making Cruise Missiles for the U.S. Military). After this, the five went underground only to re-emerge as The Wimmin's Fire Brigade. At this point they firebombed stores in the Red Hot Video chain because they claimed the chain was distributing violent porn and snuff films. On January 20, 1983, all five were arrested on the Sea-to-Sky Highway just out of Squamish, so the media dubbed them *The Squamish Five.* All were sentenced from ten years to life behind bars, but as of 2013, all five are now out of prison. Both of the women involved have written memoirs about their experiences. This graffiti appeared in an alley between Thurlow and Burrard, Robson and Haro Streets.

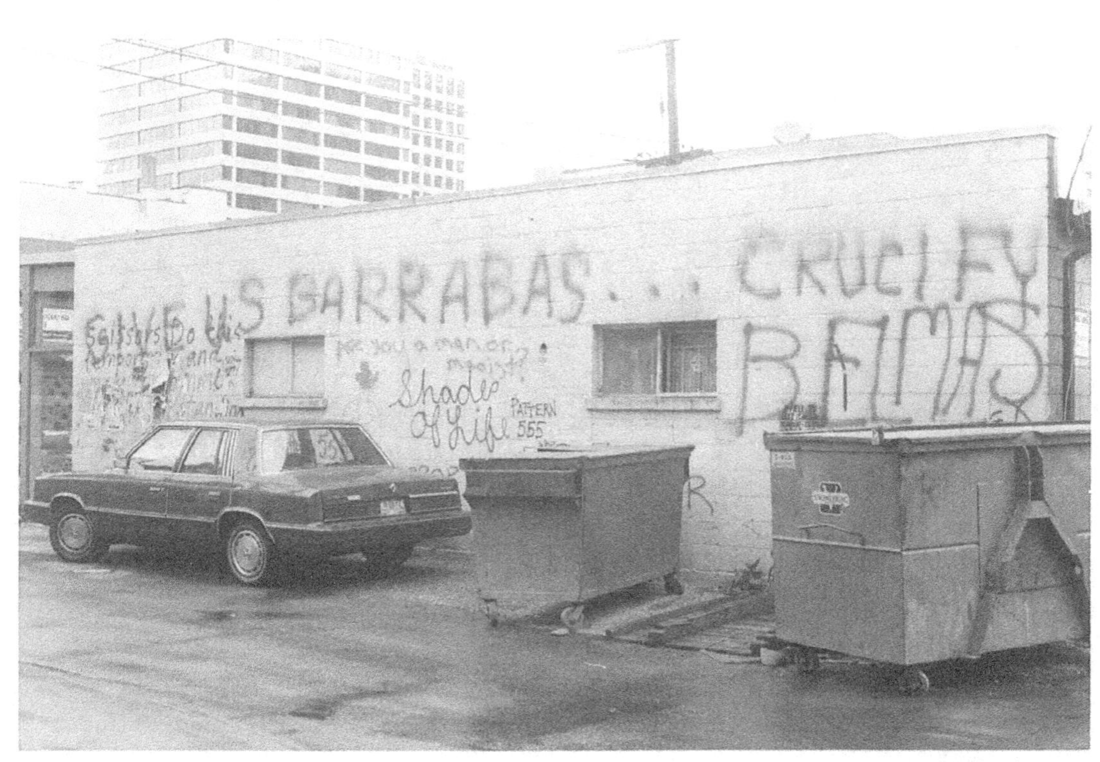
GIVE US BARRABAS . . . CRUCIFY
Shades Of Life
PATTERN 555

I found this written on the construction walls surrounding the Orillia Block on Seymour and Robson. For those who don't know, Ronald Reagan was the President of the United States throughout most of the 1980s and he was part of the conservative wave that swept the politics of the western world at that time. He was a Hollywood actor before he became the President and one of his best known movies was *Bedtime for Bonzo*.

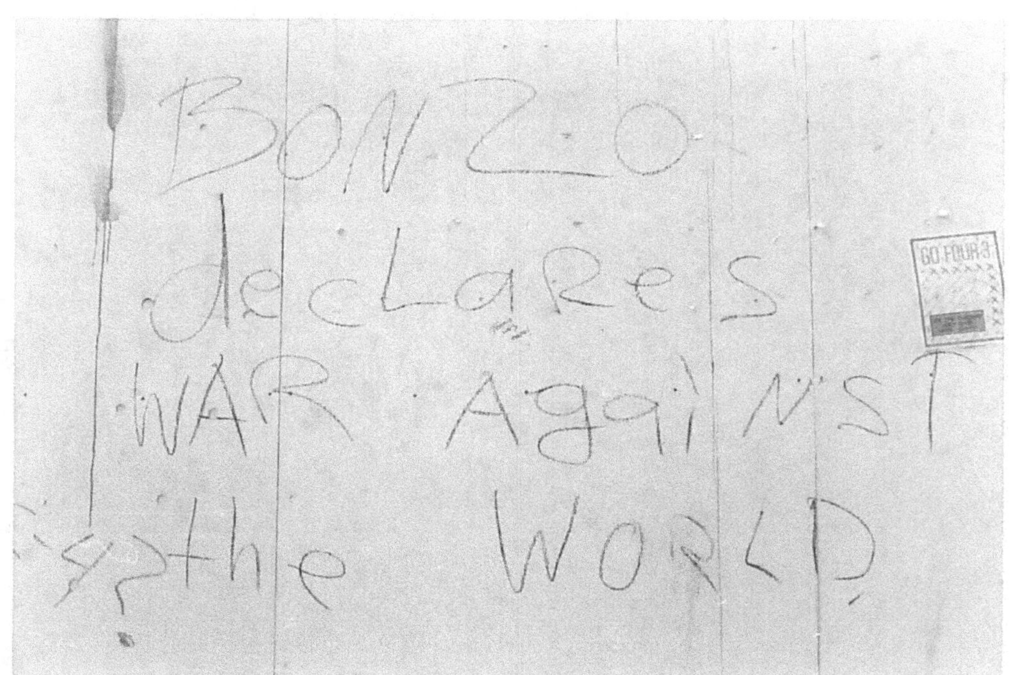

At this time Commercial Drive in Vancouver's East End, (or *The Drive*), was the center of leftist thought in Vancouver, everything was politics and politics was everything. So you saw anti-establishment sentiment scrawled across the walls of businesses on a daily basis—like this one that I found in the 1200 block of Commercial Drive.

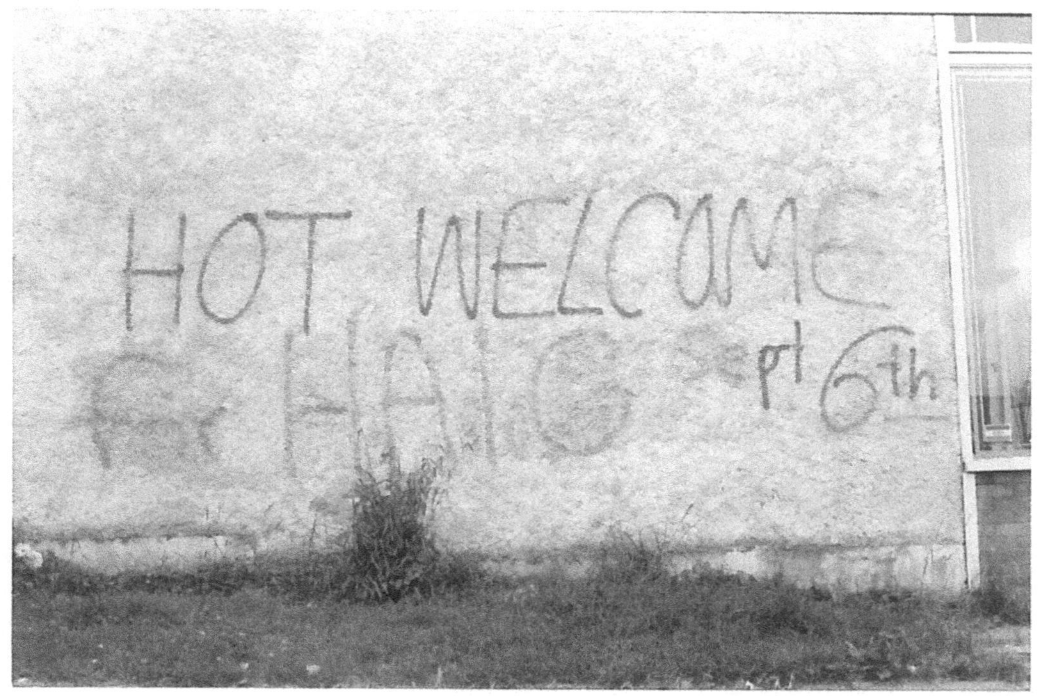

Alexander Haig was a U.S. Army General who served as White House Advisor and the American Secretary of State under Ronald Reagan during 1981 and 82. He was in Vancouver giving a speech at this time.

This was taken on Granville Street right outside of The Bay downtown while the first phase of Skytrain was still being built in 1985. At that time there was a controversy about a sewerage line being emptied into the water off of Wreck Beach. It was the talk of the town because Wreck Beach was, and still is, a popular place for people to gather in the summer.

This was written on a construction wall that was erected on Granville Island during the building of an apartment block.

If you were to stand on this corner today, (Granville and Dunsmuir), it would look totally different. This small cement wall and the handrail are still there, but those small stores you see in the background disappeared the year after this photo was taken. What presently stands there is the Vancouver flagship store for Holt Renfrew, and the addition to the Pacific Centre Mall, that was completed in 1986-87.

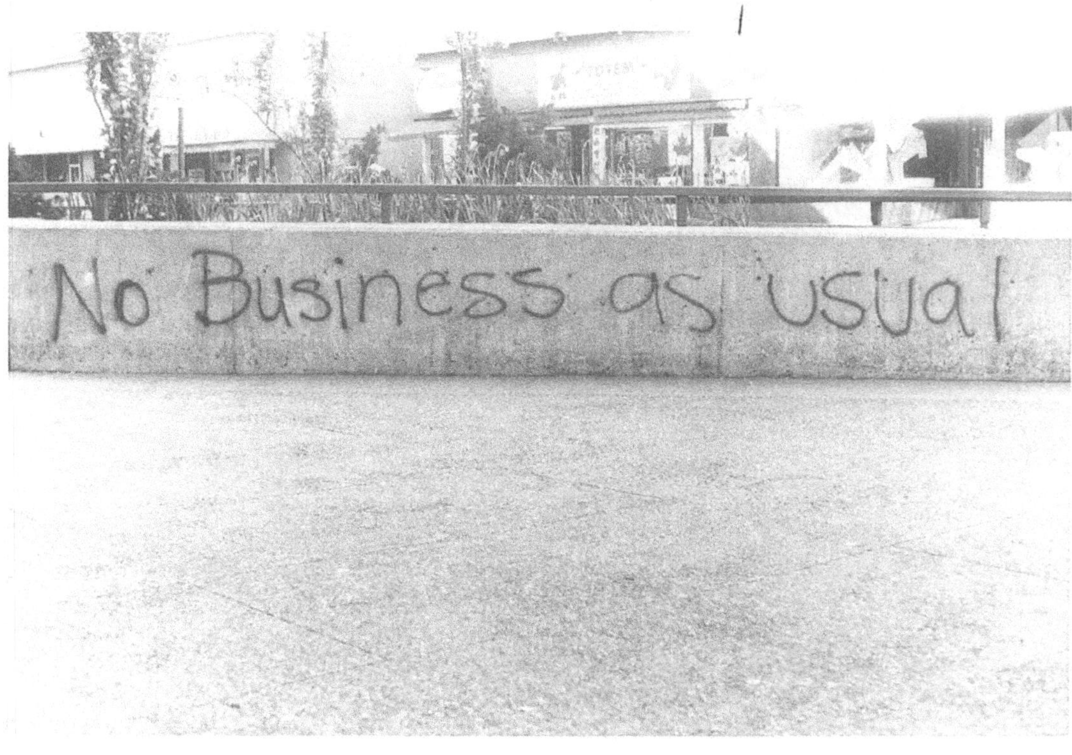

My first thought when I read this was, "Oh Really?" This was located near the corner of Burrard and Davie Streets.

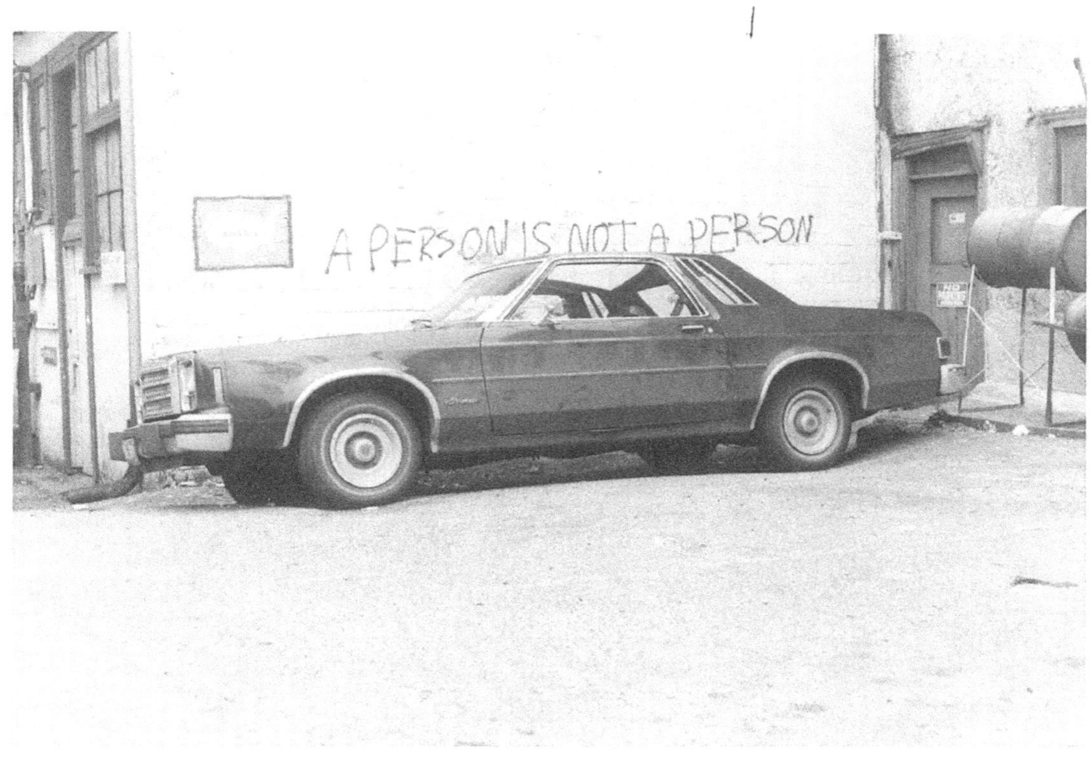

This was in the alley south of Robson Street between Thurlow and Bute. The movie Repo Man was really popular at this time.

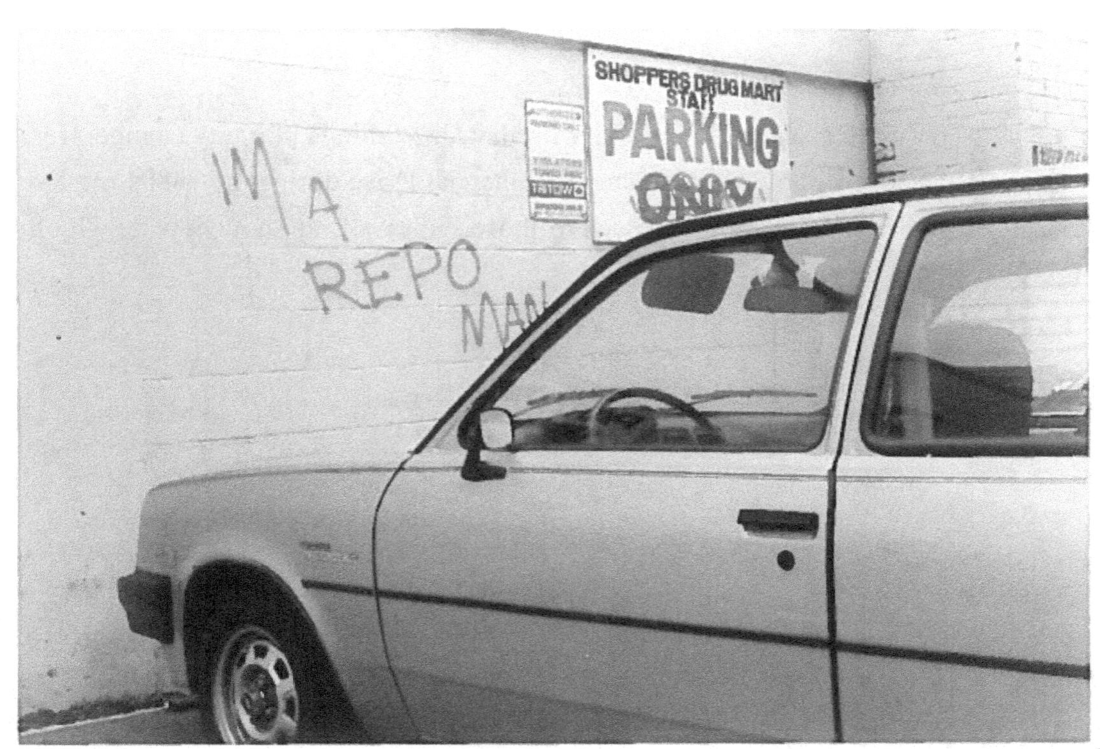
SHOPPERS DRUG MART
STAFF
PARKING
IM A
REPO
MAN

Then and Now

How time changes things and with that, how things in a city change. Here are a few photos I took along Commercial Drive during the 1980s and I've updated them by going back to those same walls to show how they look in 2013.

In the mid-eighties this was the wall of a business on the corner of East 2nd Avenue and Commercial Drive.

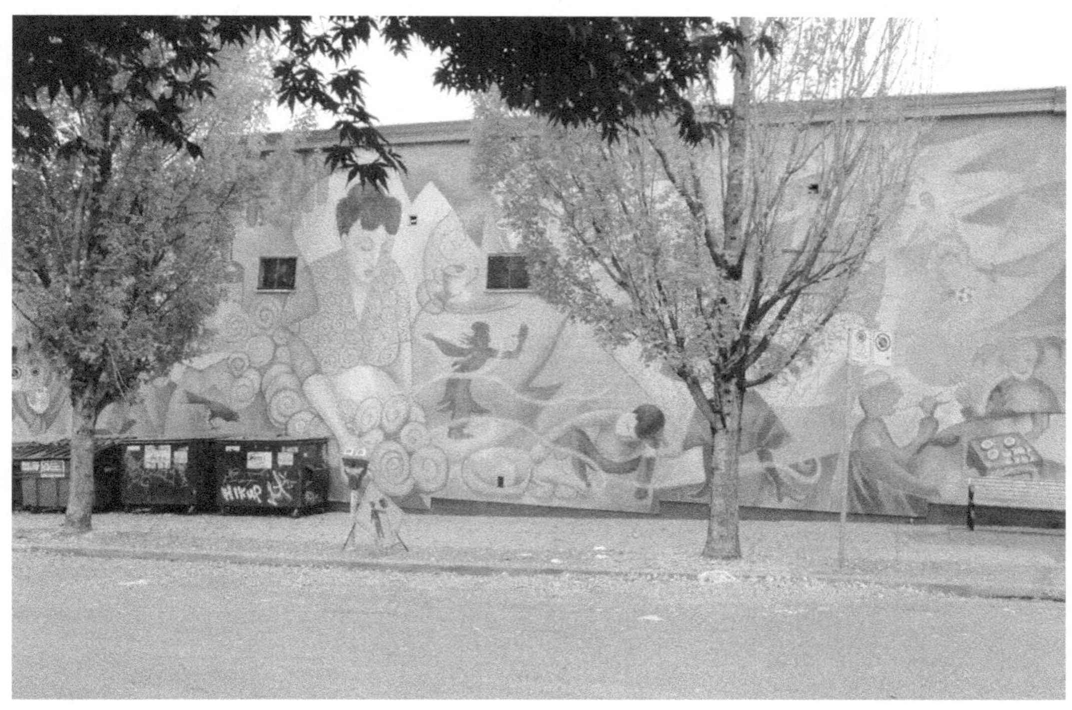

This is that same wall in 2013. Today it is the home of Fratelli's Bakery. and they commissioned this mural to be painted.

Joe's Café has always been a hot bed of politics, especially during the 1980's. As you can see, local graffiti artists couldn't resist filling the wall with their thoughts about the world at that time.

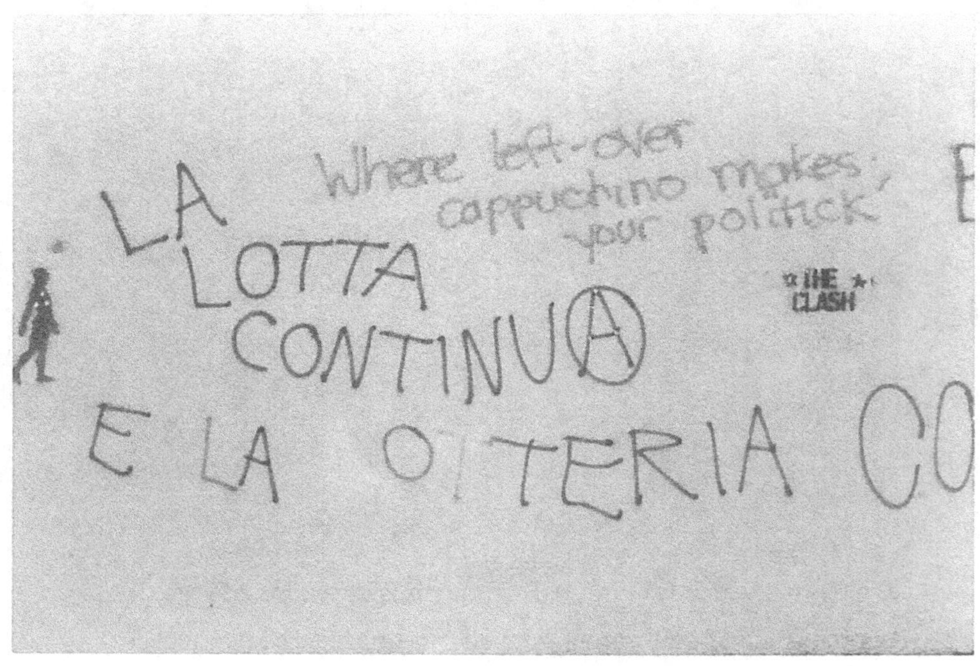

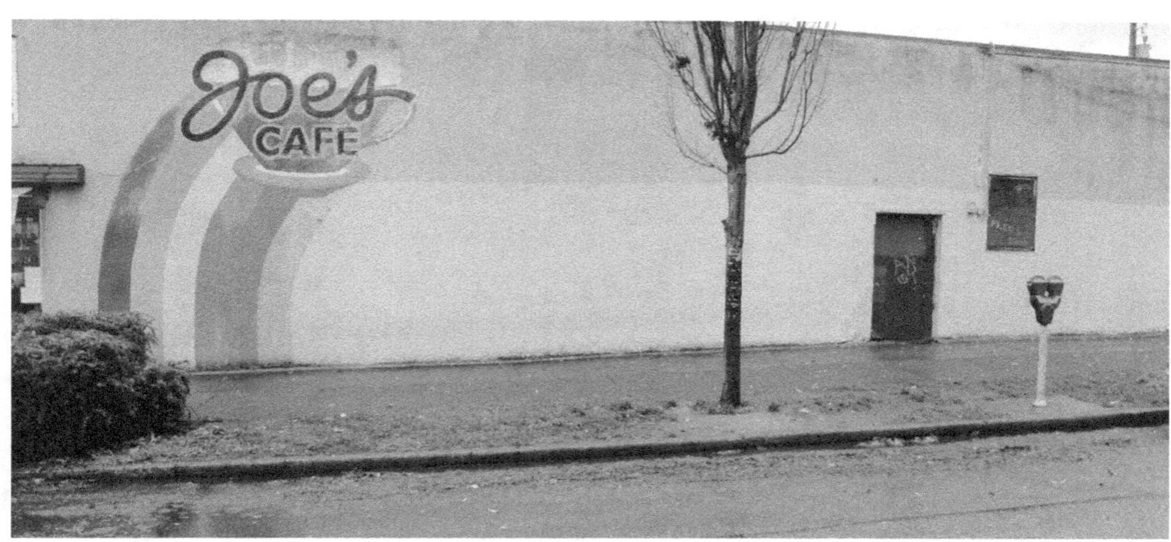

Here is the wall of Joe's Café in 2013, cleaned up and sanitized.

During the 1980's most cities of the world held a Walk for Peace every spring. Vancouver was no exception and thousands of citizens came together to march, carry banners and shout peace slogans, then they gathered at Sunset Beach for a giant Peace Rally. However, in the mid to late eighties the Walks for Peace began to wane in popularity and less people attended. Just about that time I found this piece of graffiti on the corner Commercial Drive and Kitchener Street. I mentioned to a friend what this piece of graffiti said and his only comment was, "What an interesting concept."

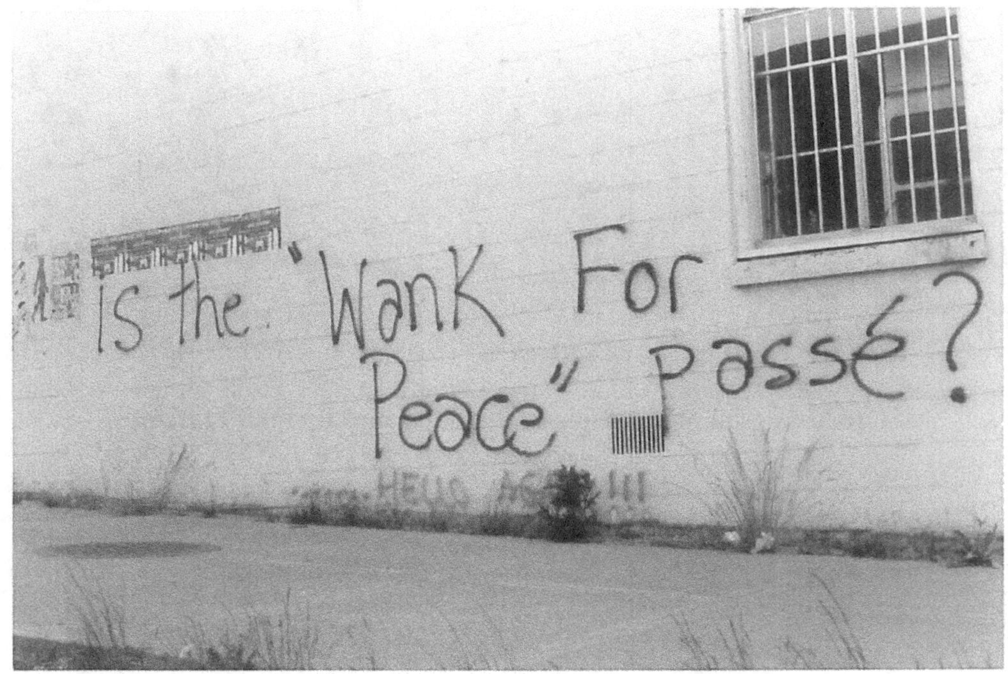

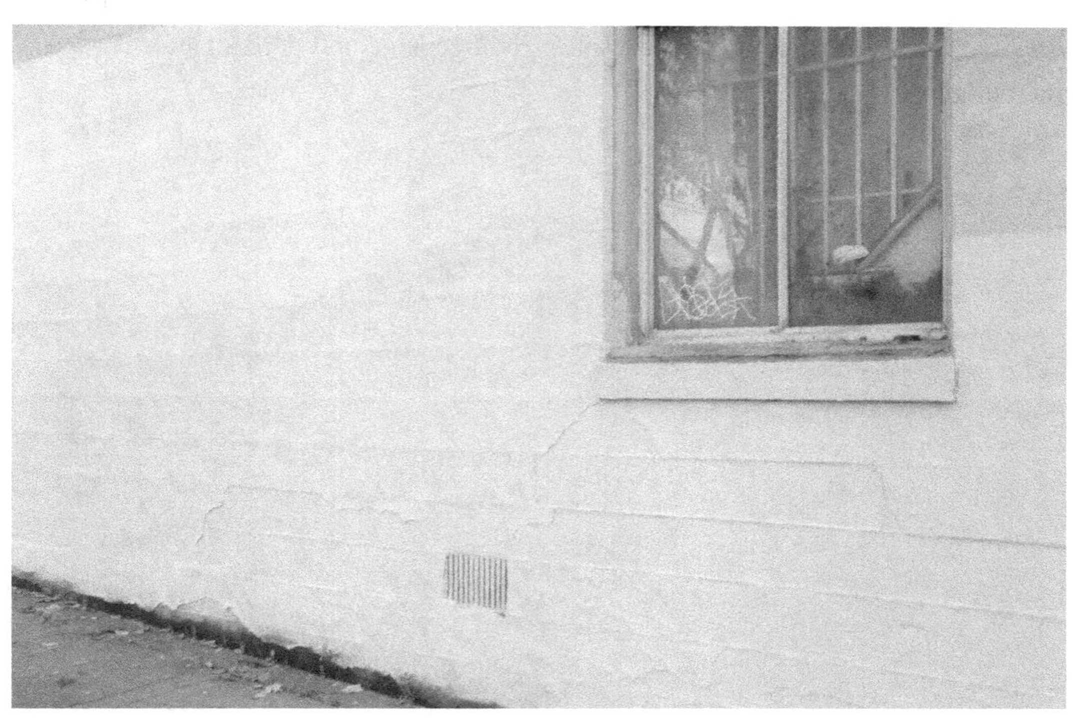

Here is that same wall in 2013, cleaned up and white washed.

This is perhaps the most dramatic difference in how a wall can look in just over twenty years. This is located on the corner of Commercial Drive and Napier Street and as you can see, politics reigned supreme in the 1980's. The US Navy is the war maker being cited here. An aircraft carrier was anchored off English Bay at this time, and as I recall it loomed large and dark silhouetted against the horizon.

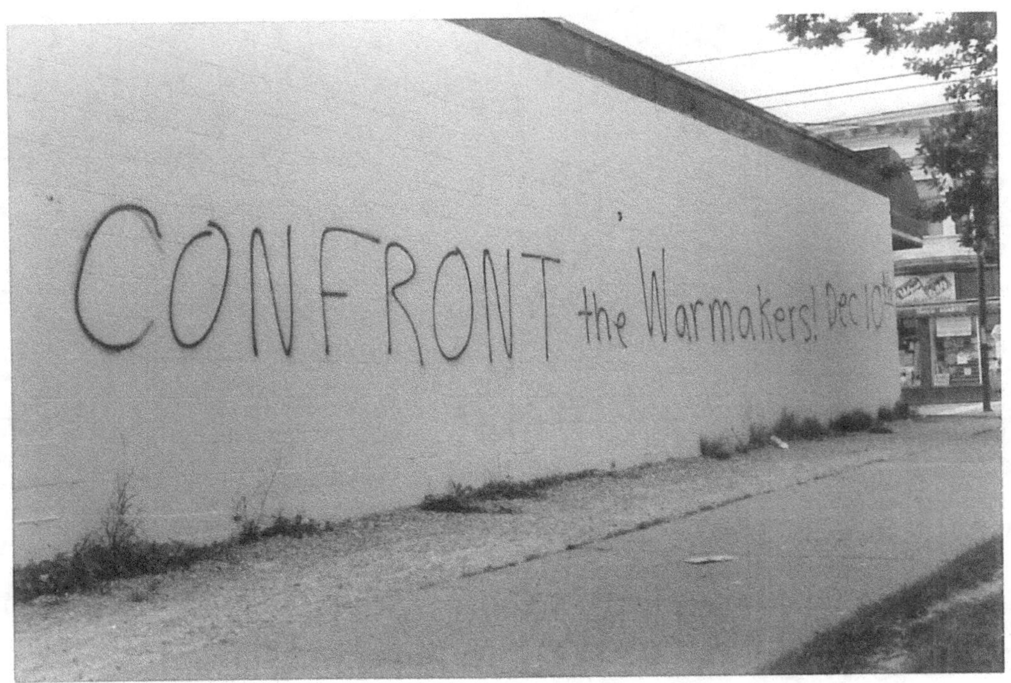

Fast forward to 2013 and the City of Vancouver has built a small park in this block of Napier Street. The street is permanently cordoned off to traffic, trees and shrubs have been planted where sidewalks once were, and park benches now occupy space where the street itself once was. And instead of political statements, a mural now adorns the wall.

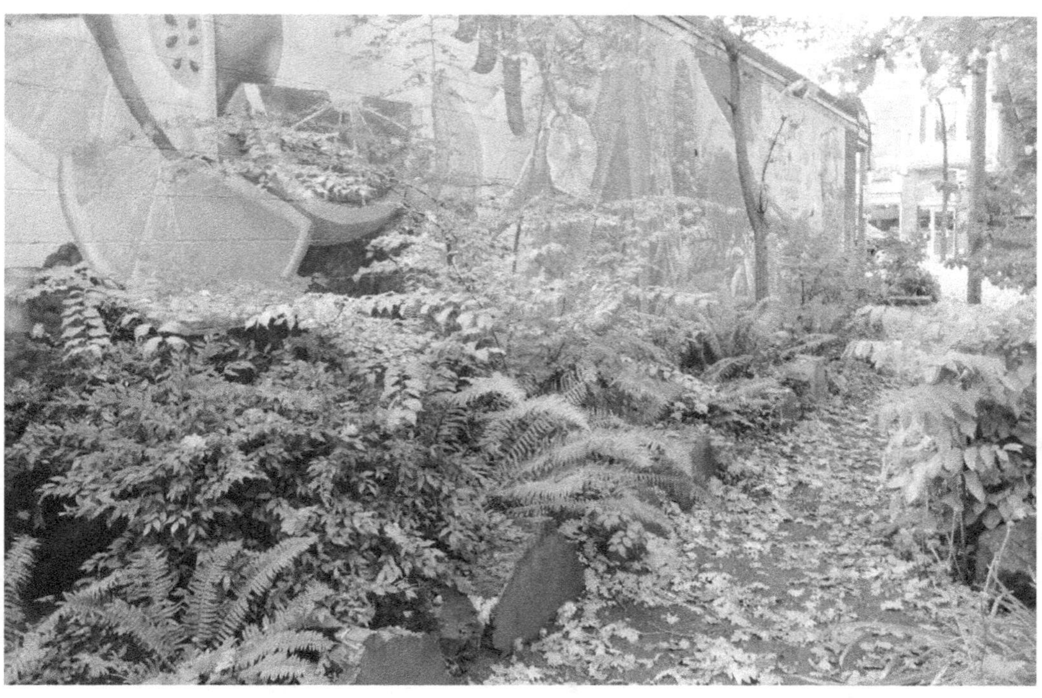

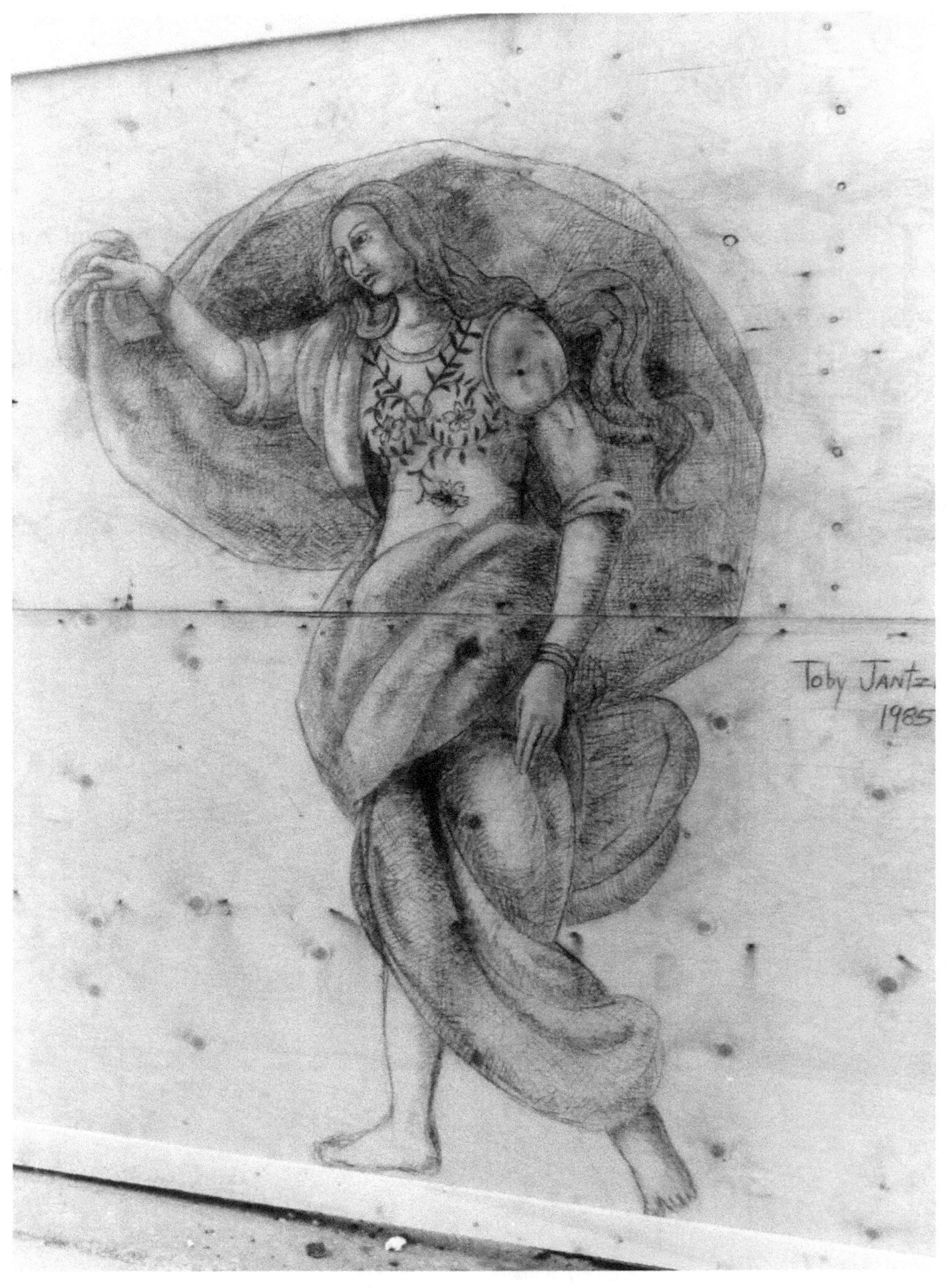

Artist: Toby Jantzen, 1985

www.ingramcontent.com/pod-product-compliance
Lightning Source LLC
LaVergne TN
LVHW080329110826
845155LV00026B/224
* 9 7 8 1 9 2 7 8 4 8 1 9 7 *